This book is lovingly dedicated to
My Daughter,

Ryan Irene

Years ago she introduced me to
Civil War Reenacting,
opening up doors to a world I never knew existed.

Thank you!

Biscuits & Bullets -

A Gettysburg Story!

By Connie Kris Hansen

Preface & Acknowledgements

Though I have never sat down and done the math, it's safe to say that I have probably made upwards of a hundred trips from Wisconsin to Gettysburg in my lifetime. My father and his love of American history first introduced me to that fair burg when I was still a little girl. It served to fuel a passion for our American Civil War that has lasted ever sense. When my daughter moved to Gettysburg around 2002 and moved into the house where Jennie was born, my excitement knew no bounds. At that time I had heard mention of Jennie Wade, but only in that vague historical sense. The full story of Jennie, Jack and Wesley came later, and by then I was spending time where Jennie was born. I walked the streets where she played, followed in her steps to St. James Lutheran Church on York and Stratton Streets where she attended services, and from there it wasn't a giant leap to writing this story.

This book is a historical novel, and as such it is not intended to be historically correct down to the last detail. It is most assuredly based on fact, but I have taken certain literary license to make the story flow where my heart wanted it to go. There is no real proof that Jack and Jennie were as close as my story has them behave, but that old adage that "absence makes the heart grow fonder," and the threat of war can make people behave in ways they might not normally do. Over time letters are lost or destroyed, memories grow dim or are distorted altogether, and we lovers of history are left with myths, half-truths, and what-might-have-been's. I am a romantic at heart, and I make no apologies for it. As such, this book has more than its share of romantic tendencies – maybe. Who really knows the hidden secrets, thoughts, or dreams of a young woman's heart? Jennie died when she was a mere twenty years old amid the heat of battle, while making bread or biscuits for hungry soldiers. Only a person with a heart big enough to share would be thus engaged. Jennie had a hard upbringing, with more than her fair share of family drama. She had every right to be cynical, hard-hearted, or even reclusive, but her actions don't speak of any of this. That being said, I allowed love to win the day and triumph in my story.

The fact that she is referred to as Jennie is one thing that has suffered much contention over the years. Since her given name is Mary Virginia Wade, it would seem to make sense that her nickname would be Ginny as opposed to Jennie. Research has shown me that various authors take a strong stand on whether to call her Jennie or Ginny, but since the major contention is "Jennie," and since it is far too late in the game to change it now, I, too, chose to stick with tradition and refer to her as Jennie.

This book has been over ten years in the making, and in that length of time I have encountered numerous people who have helped me in so many different ways, some of whom merely put up with me. My father, who is walking with Jesus even now, was the first to get me interested in the American Civil War. I don't think he had any idea where that first trip to

Gettysburg would have ultimately led me.

My sister, Terry, was a huge confidant, cheerleader, and inspirer. I don't know what I would have done without her. She tirelessly trekked all over Gettysburg with me, always offering a listening ear to my constant discussions, thoughts, and dreams about this book.

My daughter, Ryan, has helped me in ways she's not even aware of. Opening the door to Civil War reenacting and teaching me all of the ins and outs of the trade was hugely beneficial. Through her I learned the difference between thread counters, and how to avoid being caught up in the "farby" trap. A lot of what she taught me regarding everyday life in the 1860's ended up in this book.

My wonderful and patient husband, Jim, who has had to put up with me the most, deserves my heartfelt thanks and gratitude. He, too, was very patient while I prattled on about story lines, thoughts and concerns about this book. I can't thank him enough for allowing me the many trips to Gettysburg for research and family time away with my mother and sisters. I am truly blessed to have him in my life.

No list of thank you's is ever complete without thanking Mom. Year after year I dragged her back to Gettysburg to soak up the atmosphere, explore the town and battlefield, walk the streets, shop the shops, and do research for this book. She never complained, though lately she has made a point of saying, "this is the last time I'm coming back here!" She has been an absolute rock!

My son, Jayson, a history buff, a retired US Army Vet, and sometimes reenactor was hugely helpful as well. He, too, encouraged me in the writing of this book, helping me with the military aspect of the story and patiently listening to me as I rambled on about story lines and characters.

My dear sister, Joan, was bitten by the American history bug like the rest of us, and reveled in the many trips to Gettysburg in the fall. She made our many trips an absolute thrill, and encouraged me in writing this book.

Two dear friends, Dennis and Rogene Moore, were helpful in more ways than one. Not only did they encourage me in this book, but aided me in the ways of computers and publication as well. I could not have done it without their help. Not only that, but as fellow reenactors I learned much from them regarding life in the 1860"s. They are a true blessing to me.

I also need to thank Carolynn from St. James Lutheran Church. She patiently showed me around their wonderful church, happily pointing out the new and old and allowing me a glimpse of what it might have been like when Jennie attended there. I am truly grateful for her help, her knowledge, and concern for my book.

Should you wish to dig deeper into the life and times of Jennie, Jack or Wesley, there are several fine books that I recommend, and that I used during research for this one.

The first is *The Jennie Wade Story*, by Cindy L. Small. A more complete biography on Jennie cannot be found anywhere. Complete with pictures, it is the go-to- book on the three friends.

My Country Needs Me, by Enrica D'Alessandro focuses on Johnston "Jack" Hastings Skelly Jr., and like the Jennie Wade story, it contains information on all three of the friends.

Days of Darkness – The Gettysburg Civilians, by William G. Williams is a good source for knowledge on civilians in general on the events leading up to the battle, the battle itself, and events that occurred afterwards.

All that being said, I hope with all my heart that you, the reader, will enjoy this story of Jennie, Jack and Wesley.

Biscuits and Bullets...

...A Gettysburg Story

by Connie Kris Hansen

Chapter 1

1861

"Fear not, therefore;
you are of more value than many sparrows."
Matthew 10:31

"Jennie! Are you still in that book? There are wet clothes waiting in that basket by the door. Do you think they're going to dry themselves, sitting there all rolled up in that fashion? Or are you waiting for them to mold so you won't have to deal with them at all?"

Jenny let the Bible fall to her lap, shaken from her revelry by her mother's shouting. She knew her mother wasn't as mad as she pretended. There might have even been a tinge of pride, knowing her daughter was spending time reading the Bible as opposed to browsing through dime novels or some other such trash. Still, when her voice was raised, it was best to move quickly. "I'm sorry, mother. It was the Psalms, you know how I always get wrapped up in the Psalms," Jennie said by way of apology. In the next instant she was picking up the huge wicker basket of clothes.

"Psalms or not, the Good Lord only gives us so many hours of daylight to finish chores."

"I know, mother."

"Then, let's waste no more time!"

"Yes, mother." Jennie let the slamming of the screen door drowned out any further retort. After all, she had over-slept this morning, and reluctance to give up her daily devotion had put her behind.

Jennie let the clothesbasket fall to the ground with a thump. A small cloud of displaced dust drifted upward, even as she hastily extracted a freshly laundered shirt. Two strong shakes to rid it of excess water, and it was ready to hang on the line. Soon she was wrapped up in the monotony of bending, shaking, hanging, yet at the same time there was solace to be found in working alone. She reveled in her privacy, enjoying the calling of robin, thrush, and meadowlark, the warmth of sun on her neck, the scent of lilac and apple blossom, and the way the gentle breeze toyed with wayward strands of tawny hair.

Somewhere, children could be heard, shouting and laughing on their way to school. She distinctly heard one of the boys say that awful word – war! It was all anyone talked about since they had heard about the firing on Fort Sumter last week. So much had changed since then, and most of it quite literally overnight. It was the first thing on everyone's lips after "good morning, afternoon, or evening." But here, in the back yard of the family's home on Breckenridge Street, Jennie felt isolated from the rest of the world's affairs, if only momentarily. Another shake of the pillowcase and wayward drops of water sprayed her face, bringing a quick smile to the corners of her mouth and a hymn to her lips. She hummed contentedly as she worked, losing herself in thought and melody. So it was that the crisp snapping of linen in the wind drowned out the sound of approaching footsteps. Suddenly a pair of heavily calloused hands reached around and covered her eyes. "Guess who," a masculine voice demanded.

A scream of shock died before it came to fruition when she realized the voice belonged to Jack. "Hmmm," she mused, teasing him. "It can only be someone with so little regard for his life that he would sneak up on a person who is armed."

"Armed with what," he demanded, spinning her around to face him, "a clothes pin?"

"A very dangerous weapon when used in the right manner." Jenny giggled, and brandished her 'weapon' in his face.

Jack laughed, too, the smile slowly fading as his eyes darted over every inch of Jennie's face. He loved the way her eyes matched the light brown of her hair, and the way they closed part-way when she laughed, as if afraid to commit fully to anything so trivial as a joke. A blush tinged her cheeks, but whether from the chill morning or an after-effect of his little gag, he had no idea. The corners of her mouth were turned up in the remnants of a smile, and her lips were slightly parted, holding back unspoken words. Would he never get enough of staring at her face?

The silence persisted for several minutes, all the while Jack's eyes continued their tour of her face. Suddenly conscience of the image she presented, Jennie reached up and tried unsuccessfully to tame wayward wisps of hair. But it was no use, the breeze persisted in wresting it from her grasp. Soon, on that same breeze, came the sound of martial music, like some precursor of doom. And suddenly Jennie realized the awkwardness of the moment and what it held in store for her. Since the moment Jack first teased her with his "Guess who," she had known something was peculiar. After all, it was only mid morning, far too early for him to be making a social call, and Jack Skelly was nothing, if not a stickler for protocol. He wouldn't be here now, standing in her backyard when he should be at work, if it wasn't something serious. Then she saw it, that mixture of excitement and foreboding in his eyes, and she knew. Knew what he was going to say before he voiced the words.

But he voiced them anyway. "The President has asked for volunteers, and I've decided to join up. It's just for a little while, only three months, and I'll be back. Heck, it might not even take that long to teach those Southern boys a thing or two."

Jennie's shoulders sank as she sensed the determination in the man before her. But it was that underlying 'something' she couldn't put her finger on that had her mind spinning like a merry-go-round at the fair. Until she could be sure what he was about, she chose to remain silent, watching as he raised his chin in a show of bravado, false or otherwise. "You should know I've prayed about it, and I've already talked to Ma and Pa, too. They've given me their blessing, given us their blessing. Edwin's going to."

More silence as the clothes fought to free themselves from wooden bindings, and her long skirt fluttered between her legs, sometimes embracing Jack's in the bargain, making them one. It bothered her that she still couldn't read what was in those eyes, made bluer when he finally removed his hat. "Jennie," he whispered in a voice so soft it would have vanished with the wind and she would not have even known he spoke at all except that his lips moved. "Will you write to me while I'm gone? I mean, if I write first that is."

So that was it. Jack, ever the one to follow formality, knew he couldn't go to her father and ask for permission, not ever since...well, it was just out of the question, so he was unsure how to proceed.

"I've already spoken to your mother about it and she said it was all right with her," he finished.

Or did he? Suddenly it all seemed more than she wanted to bear in one morning - Jack was enlisting in the army, and her mother knew of it before she did. But that wasn't entirely true, and she knew it. The minute she heard the news of Fort Sumter and President Lincoln's call for troops she knew in her heart Jack would be first in line to sign up. The truth is, by refusing to think of it, she had hoped it would all just go away, the war, the fighting, the good-byes, all of it. But there was no refusing it any more, not with Jack standing toe to toe and staring her in the eye that way.

Unconsciously Jennie took one step backward, hoping distance would help her think more clearly. Before she could stop herself, her lips formed the thoughts of her heart. "Oh, Jack, do you have to go?"

Jack twisted the hat in his hand. "You know I do, Jennie. How could I call myself an American and not do otherwise? Would you have me stay home, safe in Gettysburg, while other men are off fighting to keep us free and united? That wouldn't be right, and I could never hold my head up and look any man in the eye knowing I didn't do my part. Besides, it's not like I'm going to be gone forever, I'll be back before summer's out. The President has only asked us to sign up for three months, and no one thinks it's going to take us any longer than that."

The look in Jack's eyes said he believed every word he just spoke, and it gave Jennie the lift her heart needed. Besides, he said he prayed about it, and she believed him. After all, she had done nothing but, since hearing of the call for troops herself.

"So, will you, Jennie?" he asked again, the twisted hat in his hand slowly losing all sense of shape.

She frowned slightly, forgetting for a moment that she hadn't answered his question about corresponding. Knowing she couldn't let him walk away seeing fear and doubt in her eyes, she forced a smile and offered him a formal curtsy, such as it was, dressed in work skirt and apron. "Of course, sir, I would be more than willing to share correspondence with you." Her words and action produced the desired results, and Jack laughed out loud.

Jennie reveled in the sweetness of that sound, but all too quickly it was replaced with the ring of martial music, louder this time. The couple instantly sobered. "That's Emil Watkins. He's too old to enlist, but not too old to fight in his own way. He got himself a small band and promises to march up and down every street in Gettysburg until everyone gets the message about the country needing volunteers."

Jennie had no reply, only praying for time and that music to cease.

"Well, I gotta get going, there's so much to do before I leave." Jack rammed the hat back on his head, harder than necessary. His eyes locked on Jennie's. "So, you'll write then?"

Jennie smiled faintly, nodding. The question was redundant, they both knew that; but the words, any words, were a means of postponing the final good-bye. Swallowing hard, Jennie asked, "When do you leave?"

The question caused Jack to break off his study of Jennie's eyes. He glanced upwards, now studying the thin, wispy clouds racing with the wind across the blue. Once more his words were almost lost to the breeze. "Two days."

Two days! Suddenly Jennie's head came alive with warring thoughts, like the battlefields she feared Jack would face. He wanted to go. She needed him to stay. What if he was hurt? Or killed? Or met someone else? There were a thousand questions she wanted answers to. The least of which was, would he really be back in three months? His face didn't look so positive now.

Impulsively Jennie threw her arms around Jack in a strong embrace. "Then go with God and know He'll be watching over you." With that, she broke free and made a dash for the back door. "I'll write to you, Jack Skelly!" she called over her shoulder before the slamming of the door cut off her words.

Inside, she ran for the nearest window, determined for one last look at this man she had called friend for as far back as she could remember. Fortunately he couldn't see her, standing in the shadows near the curtain. He stood there, still as a soldier at attention, his eyes locked on the back door, where she had recently disappeared. She wondered what he was thinking, standing there, alone in the yard, with drying clothes flapping a make-shift salute in the stiff breeze. Was he angry over her abrupt departure? Or did he understand her need to get away before the first tears fell? Did he think her rude, unfeeling, uncaring? Did he think she didn't....love him? Jennie's hand flew to her mouth, stifling a gasp of shock. Love? She had never uttered that word to Jack before. Was it too late now? Should she say such a thing while he was facing the hordes of a Southern army? Was the feeling real, or was it merely the thought of good-bye? The passage of time escaped her as she fought a private battle in her head. Yet all the while, Jack stood resolutely in the yard, staring at the door, as if willing her to come back.

Dashing a tear from her cheek, Jennie made up her mind. She sprinted for the back door, her smile growing wider as determination made each step quicker than the one before. Wooden floorboards squeaked in rebellion, and the back door screamed out in protest when Jennie forced it open. Quickly her eyes took in the scene, her feet and smile slowing as recognition sank in. The sounds were just as before, martial music fading in the distance, robins and jays calling out to mates, and the hurried clomping of horses hooves racing down the street. But where was Jack? A quick glance around revealed nothing but a garden patch in desperate need of attention, lilac blooms swaying with the breeze, and a half empty wicker basket on the ground. Even the clothes on the line seemed to mock her as they cheerfully waved farewell, something she wasn't able to do now, because...Jack was gone.

May 15, 1861
York, Penn

Dear Jennie,

I did not want the opportunity to pass by allowing me to wish you a happy birthday. I am not sure if you will get this letter on time or not because I do not know how well the mail is getting through, but I thought I would try. How are things with you and everyone in town? You must promise to write and tell me all of the news. How did you spend your birthday? Did your mother make you a cake? I don't have any news to report. My company is still in York and we spend our days drilling, marching, and drilling some more. It is tiresome, but they promise us that soon we will get our chance to teach those boys down south a lesson they won't soon forget. We are all in fine spirits and looking forward to that day. The food here is first rate and I think I am even gaining some weight. Mostly we eat beef or bacon, desiccated vegetables, coffee and something they call hardtack. It is a sort of hard cracker or biscuit with no flavor, though the weevils, worms and bugs seem to like it well enough. The men have taken to call it by other names, like worm castles or teeth dullers. It is near impossible to eat plain, but if you dunk it in coffee first it will go down all right.

Tell me of news of home. I cannot believe that everything is the same as before Ft. Sumter was attacked. The feelings amongst the men here is mostly split between those that think we will teach those southern boys a lesson real quick, and those that think the world is near coming to an end. They think there will be a great war coming soon. I think they are wrong and that once those Secesch see how strong we are and how many we are, they will run like scared deer and we will win the day. But however it goes, I will stay until the end.

The bugle has just sounded the call for mess, so I must go now or will surely miss out. Jennie, I hope you had a happy birthday and wish that I was there to say it to your pretty face. Give my best regards to you, your family, and all of our dear friends at home. Write soon.

From Your Dear Friend,
Jack

Gettysburg
July 25, 1861

My Dear Jack,

We have just heard the awful news about a terrible battle. They are calling it Bull Run and they say that there are hundreds of dead and wounded soldiers. Though I am so very sad to hear the news, I am glad that you were not there to take part in it. I know that is a selfish thing to say, but I cannot help myself. I have grown very selfish towards you ever since this war began. I wonder now, do you still think it will be over in a few months?

The Ladies at church are forming a committee to gather socks, shirts, bandages, and other needful items to package up and send to our troops. I will go tomorrow afternoon to see how I might be of service.

I saw Annie Culp on the street the other day and asked if she has heard anything from Wesley and she said no. I cannot help but wonder if she would tell me the truth or not because there are those in town that think ill of him right now. He did not come back to join the Federal cause like you and the rest of the boys from Gettysburg, so they are calling him a traitor. Our Wesley, a traitor! I can scarce believe it. Do you remember how much fun we used to have skimming stones across Rock Creek, going fishing, having picnics in the meadow on his uncle's hill? What happened to those days, Jack? I wish I had them in a box or bottle now so that I could take them out, one by one, and relive them all over again. Isn't that shameful of me? If I held onto the past that way, how would I ever find out what the future had

15

in store? But the future can be very scary, especially with a war going on. Promise me you will take care of yourself, Jack, and come home to me when it is all over.

I'm sorry for going on this way. I think it is all of the latest news about the battle that has me so maudlin. I will try and be more cheery in my next letter, but still promise me you will stay safe. Until then, I remain your most affectionate friend.

Jennie

Jennie swept the last of the dirt out the back door just as her little brother, Harry, clambered in, shoes dirty, and water dripping from the pail he was carrying to the stove. With hand on hip she gave him her fiercest scowl, a scowl that didn't earn her the desired results, as six-year old Harry simply tossed his brightest smile her way. She knew her point had gotten across, however, when he didn't venture any farther into the house, but hustled right back out the door from whence he came. Another few swipes and the latest intrusion of dirt also found its way outside. Jennie let go of the urge to simply stay outside where a cool breeze toyed with the hem of her long skirt, begging her come out and play, as in days of yore. Those wonderful days of childhood, when she, Jack, Wesley, and others would run the streets, fields and hills of Gettysburg, screaming and laughing, as if they didn't have a care in the world. And they didn't really, not back then.

The Wade family had never had much money, she realized, but children are slow to pick that up. All that little children are aware of is food on the table, an occasional sweet, friends to play with in the daytime, and sisters and brothers to play with in the evening. At least, that was her world back then. But now, at seventeen, she was a grown woman, with grown-up responsibilities. There were still five people living in this small, clapboard house on Breckenridge Street. There was their mother, Mary Wade, her older sister, Georgia, herself, and two younger brothers, John, who was fifteen, and little Harry, only six years old. And all of them pitched in to keep a sturdy roof over their heads.

A shout from the newsboy on the corner caught her attention just before the back door closed tight on her childhood revelries. It was the war again, she knew. It was all that anyone talked about any more, whether at church, in the square, or at the market, "have you heard the latest from Washington City?" Why, the war has already raged on for one month longer than they said it would when all of our eligible young men volunteered for President Lincoln's Three Month War. Jennie found her head beginning to explode with the injustice of it all when a shout from the next room brought her on the run.

Dashing through the kitchen and sitting room, she entered the room set aside as their tailor shop on the run. Complete with its own entrance to the outside, it was perfect for conducting business with clients, and keeping everything to do with their tailoring trade all in one place. The scene that greeted her eyes was almost comical, and all thoughts of war were instantly forgotten. Her mother and older sister were both on their knees, fannies high in the air as they worked to retrieve straight pins that had scattered across the wood floor. Georgia, her sister, was silent, but her mother was mumbling under her breath about this being the umpteenth time today they have had to put their sewing on hold just to gather up pins and put them back in the jar.

Georgia let out a small yelp when she inadvertently found a wayward pin with her knee.

"Don't move, George! I see it," called out Jennie, as she hastily removed the pin from the folds of Georgia's skirt. A few moments later and the rest of the pins were back in the jar where they belonged.

"Thank you, Jennie," Georgia offered before retrieving her chair by the window. She glanced at her mother to gage her anger and realized that all was well, now that the catastrophe was once more behind them.

Jennie stepped over a pile of discarded scrap cloth carelessly tossed on the floor in order to tie back the lace curtain that continued dancing in the breeze from the open window. Its long, exuberant tail seemed to be the culprit responsible for knocking over the pin jar this time, and since it was simply too warm to work with the window closed, the lace would have to be contained. She tied it in a gentle knot, knowing the weight would keep it under control now.

"Do you two need any help in here," Jennie offered the pair.

"Well, since we have a bit of time before we need to start dinner, why don't you spell your sister for a few minutes. She has been a bit over wrought ever since she heard them shouting that the mail has arrived." Mary Wade's eyes never left the trim she was painstakingly sewing on the bottom of a skirt, her arthritic fingers purposefully pulling the needle and thread in and out.

Jennie, listening to the cries as well, glanced out the window and saw the throng of people gathering around the stage on the corner of Breckinridge and Baltimore Streets. The arrival of mail had always brought an eager crowd to the corner, but more so these days, with so many of the towns people, men in particular, gone to far off places.

Georgia, busy sewing the same trim on the bodice of the dress, let it fall into her lap as she looked pleadingly at her sister.

Jennie smiled, walked the few steps across the room, and relieved her sister of her task. "I was going to get started on the some of the mending projects, but I believe they can keep for a little while yet."

The few words had barely left her mouth before Georgia was out on the street, the front door slamming a good-bye behind her.

Jennie, wishing she had gone with her sister to see about a letter for herself as well, instead picked up the discarded bodice, her seamstress eyes expertly noticing where her sister left off, and where she was going with the trim.

Her mother, still intent on her own task, knew the thoughts of her youngest daughter. "You know George will bring back any letters that might have arrived from Jack for you, don't you? She's just so anxious to hear from Louis these days. In his last letter he promised to try and come home on leave so they could be married, but of course he can't give her a date yet, and might not be able to until almost the last minute. It's hard on her."

"I know, Mama, and I hope she hears from Louis real soon. I am just having a hard time imagining life in this house without her around all the time."

Mary Wade laughed softly. "Wait until you're a mother yourself. You'll quickly learn that you cannot hold onto your children forever. You give birth to them, you love them to pieces, and they take a piece of your heart with them every time they walk out the door."

The house grew silent as the two women put needle to cloth. The breeze, such a nuisance before, suddenly seemed to have lost enough strength to filter the lace curtain at all. Jennie wiped her brow with a hankie. Her mother did the same, taking a momentary break from her sewing. Stretching her fingers and trying to work life back into them, she carried on her conversation. "It seems harsh of me, I know, but I can't help realizing that I am going to miss more of Georgia than just her presence in the house. I'm going to miss the money she brings in by helping in the tailor shop. I know it's one less mouth to feed, but she doesn't eat enough to keep a bird alive anyway, no, she brought in more than she took out of this household, bless her!"

Her mother seemed close to tears, and before Jennie could think of some comforting words to offer, her younger brother, John, came bounding into the room, out of breath and holding onto the door jam to keep from falling headlong onto the floor. "I want to join the cavalry!"

September 30, 1861
Camp Buehler Lutherville, Maryland

Dear Jennie,

By now you have probably heard that I have reenlisted in the army. It seemed the only patriotic thing to do, as this war is by no means over and I have always said that I will see it through to the end. My new term will expire in three years, but I will reenlist again if I have to. You have doubtless heard what my mother feels about my situation, but I would rather endure her tears than the shame I would bring upon my family and my country by giving up and coming home. I know it is hard on her, as my brother, Ed, and our

Pa, too, has signed on, but it is all for the best, I think.

Our new camp, Camp Buehler, is named after our elected commander. I don't know that much about him yet, but he seems first rate and most of the men like him. We have been assigned to guard the railroad, but I don't know for how long. They never tell us anything, except for when to wake up, when to sleep, when to eat, when and how far to march. We still do a lot of drilling and we are starting to look real good on the field. Notwithstanding how busy we are, it is still boring work. We march in place, we march in a line, we march in the rain, and we march in the sun. Sometimes, when we get back to our tent all I want to do is sleep, but I know that you will appreciate a letter now and then, so I make sure I set aside time for that. Your letters help me get through the day, too. I keep them all and reread them whenever I get the chance. Some of the other men like to play cards, or invent games of skill just to have something to bet on, but I don't do any of that. You don't have to worry about me on that score.

Another thing I do is mending for some of the men. My Pa taught me a right smart service there, though I didn't much appreciate it at the time. I have done several different mending jobs now for money and was able to send it all home to mother. She spoke of you in her last letter to me. She said she ran into you on the street and that you both shared a few words. I wish I was there to share a few words with you now. What would we talk about, I wonder. Certainly we would talk about the weather, because today was a good day for a walk. But even if it was raining, it would be a good day for a walk with you.

A lot of the men are already thinking ahead to Christmas

and hoping to get leave to go home. I am one of those men, but I do not think it is going to happen. Jim J. got word that his little boy died and they wouldn't give him leave to go be with his family. If they don't let you home for such times as that, I don't think that yearning hearts at Christmas will win out. Still, I don't think this war can go on too much longer, so we will soon be home at any rate. Tell everyone you meet that I send greetings, and keep a double dose of "greetings" for yourself. Until the next time.,

I remain your most trusted friend,
Jack

Gettysburg
December 10, 1861

Dear Jack,

Can Christmas really be almost upon us? It certainly feels like it outside, but my inner being says that it can't be so. I have always loved and looked forward to Christmas, but this year seems like such a bleak one. Of course, I am not referring to a lack of bounty, Christmas presents, or a table groaning from the weight of too much food. I am talking about the lack of friends we will be privileged to share the day with. Too many are gone, like you, to parts unknown, and others are gone forever, even now lying in the cemetery outside of town. But I should not be going on this way, not to you, who probably feels the loss of the holiday even more than me.

Instead, I will tell you of my brother John, and the fright he gave Mama and me a few months back. I don't know why I didn't think to tell you sooner, but Mama and I were sewing together, working on a new dress for Mrs. Stemplenik, when John announced that he wanted to join the cavalry. Well, you can imagine Mama's reaction to such news coming from her fifteen-year old son. He argued that other boys his age were joining up and he wanted to be a part of it. Mama said no, of course, but promised she would consider it when he came of age. By then we hope that this whole war will be over and we won't have to hear talk of him joining the army at all.

Did you know that Georgia is engaged to be married? She and Louis McClellan are making plans as soon as he can get away from the army for a few days. I think he called it "going on leave." They wanted to be married before Christmas, but now think it might have to wait until spring. Mama is worried about losing George's skilled sewing fingers in the tailor shop, but she won't say anything to her about it naturally. She says we all have to grow up and make our own way eventually, and The Good Lord will provide for her just as He always has. She is right to think that, too, because I am already looking into something that might help us. I have heard about a new lady in town. Her name is Hilda Brinkerhoff and she has a young crippled son who needs looking after while she works outside of town during the week. She is willing to pay us to board him while she is away, so that money will come in real handy. Besides the money, he will make a good playmate for our little Harry, who is six-years old now. Can you believe it? It seems like only yesterday that he was a baby crawling on the floor!

I will have a surprise for you soon, and I hope you will like it. Is it a surprise even if I tell you what it is? I think this surprise will be, because even if I tell you what it is you won't know what it looks like until you receive it. So now I will tell you that Georgia, Maria and I are to have our likenesses taken later this week. Maria set the appointment at a photography shop over on Chambersburg Street near the diamond. It was Georgia's idea, but the rest of us quickly agreed. I will send you a daguerreotype as soon as I have one and hope that you will find it a most pleasant surprise. Have I told you before how much comfort it gives me to have your likeness with me at all times? I carry it in my pocket and take it out to look at it – you – any time the mood strikes me. Your letters, too, I read so often I'm afraid they will simply fall apart at the creases!

What do you think of the new general for the army – General George McClellan? Our Georgia thinks he is wonderful and only wishes that her Louis, also named McClellan, was a relation. He isn't, of course, but that doesn't stop her from wishing it.

Our church is doing something different this season. Instead of having a Christmas bazaar and using the money for beautifying the church and helping the local poor, we are going to give all of the proceeds to our soldiers. Besides money, we are knitting socks and mittens, sewing shirts, rolling bandages, and making any number of useful items for our boys so far from home. I promised to be there tomorrow to help make up the packages. We are hoping against hope that the packages will arrive in time for the soldiers Christmas Day celebration. As for me, all I would need to make my day happy would be to see you standing on my stoop. If not that, then a letter would be the next best thing. When a week goes by and I don't hear from you, I sometimes think I will just go crazy!

Now I must go, as Mrs. Westmore will be here soon with the latest copy of Godey's magazine. She is so nice to let Mama, Georgia and me look at the latest fashion plates and read the stories and articles at the back. It is full of helpful receipts, hints and tips for running a well-run household. I am sure that you would not find it so, but we ladies like it very much. Please be careful with yourself, Jack, and know that I am praying for you and that Our Good Lord is always watching over you. Let me hear from you again soon.

I remain your most devoted friend and admirer,

Jennie

Early morning sunshine poured through the kitchen window at the two-story house on Breckinridge Street. The Wade family was sitting around their much-abused wooden kitchen table, savoring the last of their tea before starting their day. Jennie glared at the dust motes dancing in the light of the streaming sun, wishing they would simply follow it right back outside from whence it came.

Harry, never one to sit still for any length of time, was doing his best to imitate his older brother, John, by teetering his chair on its two back legs. John, quite aware of the situation, tilted his chair back still farther, all the while pretending he hadn't noticed Harry's glances in his direction. Suddenly there was a loud crash as little Harry's chair went tumbling over backwards, carrying its charge with it. Harry let out a squeal, while John roared with laughter.

Mrs. Wade was on her feet in an instant. Tossing her napkin angrily on the table she made a move towards John, but he had anticipated her action and was on his feet heading for the door. "Sorry, Ma, I'll be late for school!" John grabbed his coat from its hook by the door and was turning the knob, making good his escape, when her words stopped him in his tracks.

"John James Wade! You will wait for your brother so he doesn't have to walk to school alone this day! This is all your doing, and you knew very well where its outcome might lead from the moment you tilted that chair of yours back in the first place! I swear I don't know where these notions of yours come from sometimes, but the day is soon coming..."

The rest of her words were lost in the closing of the door. Jennie had helped Harry to his feet and into his coat. He was none the worse for wear, sporting a bruised ego more than a bruised body as he trudged after John in the cold winter air. She watched for a moment as he caught up with his brother. John tussled his hair playfully, and said something to him she couldn't hear. Whatever it was, it earned John a poke in the ribs, and then both boys took off on a run down the street.

Jennie closed the door, leaning on it for a moment while she remembered her own school days. It really wasn't all that long ago, as she thought about it. Looking back now, she realized they weren't all that care free as they seemed to John and Harry right now. She had to rise earlier than normal if she wanted to read a few lines from her Bible before starting the day. After that she had to help Mama with breakfast, and there was always work in the tailor shop waiting for her when she returned home. She wondered how she ever found time for schoolwork and passing grades at all! Granted, her schoolwork wasn't first rate, but at least she had passed, which is more than she could say for some of the others in school. Harry was too young to show more than a spark of promise, but John was already exhibiting that attitude of boys his age, that school is just a waste of time. His mind, and probably his heart, was set on the army and the war. It bothered her, and her mother too, to no end, that a war being fought so far away was touching so many lives so close to home. She knew it was just a matter of time before John brought up enlisting again. No matter the schoolboy smile on his face when he left home this morning, there were a man's thoughts swirling around in that head.

Pushing herself away from the door, Jennie grabbed a rag to wipe crumbs from the kitchen table. She had barely collected them in her hand when a knock at the door brought her up short. The knock came at the tailor shop door, so it was business, not visitors. A quick glance over her shoulder revealed her mother elbow deep in dishwater, while Georgia, rag in hand, was putting dishes away on a top shelf.

"I'll see who it is," Jennie announced, wiping her hand on her apron as she headed for the tailor room door. An impatient knock sounded again, and Jennie instinctively picked up her pace. "Coming," she called out. And as she took the last few steps her mind raced over whom she might expect, because there were no fittings scheduled as far as she knew. Curiosity propelled her forward, but nothing prepared her for the shock she received upon opening the door. A soldier, dressed in a blue Union uniform stood on their stoop, hat in hand, and a bundle under his arm. A cold draft of air raced across her face, taking her breath away and any words she might have uttered with it into the room.

The soldier was the first to speak. "I'm sorry to bother you, Ma'am," he said," but I was told that you might be able to help me with some mending I need doing." When Jennie didn't respond fast enough, he continued. "I'm with the Porter Guards. Ah, that is, well, I mean, I'm with 10th New York Cavalry,

Ma'am, and we're going to be wintering here in town for a few months and this here uniform of mine could really use some patching up. A man at the dry goods store said that you take in mending and might be able to help me out. Are you willing?"

Thoughts of Jack were quickly dispelled as Jennie finally found her voice. "Oh, I'm so sorry to leave you standing in the cold that way. Won't you come in?" Jennie stepped aside so the soldier could enter the tailor shop. He was young, quite tall, with blonde hair combed back straight back from his forehead. His eyes were blue, shy, and it seemed to take all the nerve he could muster up to utter the few words he just did. Except for the wearing of a blue uniform, he bore no resemblance to Jack whatsoever, but then, it didn't take much to conjure up images of Jack in Jennie's mind. Suddenly her mind was over occupied with thoughts of Jack, his whereabouts, his health, what he was doing, how long before the day would come when she would see *him* standing on her stoop. Silent moments passed until she became aware of the soldier holding out a neatly wrapped bundle for her inspection. Pretending a cough to hide the awkwardness of the moment, Jennie forced a quick smile. "My apologies. What do we have here?"

Setting the bundle on a nearby table, Jennie expertly opened it and held the uniform up for inspection. The first thing that struck her was the odor. It smelled of campfire, perspiration, dirt, and food aromas she couldn't quite identify. The knees were worn nearly straight through on the trousers, with a button dangling by a mere thread. The jacket had a gaping hole beneath one arm and was so dirty she shuttered to handle it any more than necessary for fear of the dirt that might accumulate on the tailor room floor.

The soldier hadn't said a word since entering the shop, but he'd seen the pause that briefly registered on Jennie's face over the condition of his uniform. "I guess I should have seen the camp laundress before bringing it into town, but I..."

"That's all right, we can take care of that for you, too.

Why don't you come back in a day or two and we should have it all ready for you. Would that suit you?"

"Oh, yes, Ma'am, that would be first rate. Thank you kindly, Ma'am. Um, if it's all right with you, that is, if you don't mind, would it be all right if I told some of the other boys about your establishment here? There's a whole passel of us what could use with a good lot of mending."

"Certainly! That would be wonderful, we'd be glad to help. Tell them to come anytime." And with that, Jennie saw the soldier to the door, her thanks to God for sending this additional blessing their way already going up in prayer.

January 1, 1862

Camp Buehler
Lutherville, Maryland

Dear Jennie,

Can you believe that another year has come and gone already, and what changes it has wrought. I remember the fun we had last year at this same time and look forward to when we can have that fun again. But for now I will stay the course, march and drill, and do whatever I have to do to preserve the Union. Last night things got pretty quiet for awhile while everyone was lost in their own thoughts of home. Mostly we were thinking of the past, I think, until someone said that he couldn't wait to kill him some Rebs and get this war over so he could go home for good. It got me to thinking real hard, about killing someone, I mean. It was easy enough when I first signed on to talk about killing the enemy, killing them all if that's what it took to get this war over with, but now I'm sitting here wondering. I'm wondering if I can point my musket at someone, pull the trigger and watch him die. And even if I think I'm capable of doing it, I wonder what you would think of me then. Would you still think fondly of me, call me friend, would you still love me?

I received your letter about George getting married. That is wonderful news, to be sure! I know Louis, and he is a good sort. They will make a fine family I think. I know someone else who would make a fine family some day, too. Don't you just want to guess who!

Tell John for me not to be too quick to sign on. War is great to talk about around the fire at night or with the boys in the street, but it is not all it is cracked up to be. It is more tedious marching, drilling, eating poor food, and being lonely amidst hundreds of men than whatever glamour might come of it. It is true that I have not seen the elephant yet (that is a phrase we use to mean being in battle for the first time) but I cannot imagine that it will make up for months of sitting around idle. Your mother is right to tell him to wait until he is of age. Maybe by then it will all be over and he will never have to endure what I have endured.

It is right cold here at night now, and drinking coffee to

warm up before going to bed is not the answer. But I have to say that I do sleep comfortably with my blanket wrapped tightly around me, and my gum blanket on top of that. My gum blanket helps to keep the dampness away and comes in real handy when we have to sleep outside. But right now we have snug little cabins that hold about six to eight men each. They are crowded and can get real noisy at times, but at least I have my own bed, and it is out of the weather. I have learned to make do.

I am sorry if this letter seems so short. I hear singing coming from somewhere outside and think some of the fellows are trying to lift their sodden spirits. I believe I will join them. Please give my best to your family and all those you meet on the streets of our fair town of Gettysburg.

I remain your devoted friend,
Jack

Chapter 2

1862

"God is our refuge and strength, a very
present help in trouble. Therefore we will not fear,
though the earth be removed, and though the
mountains be carried into the midst of the sea."
Psalm 46:1-2

The Wade household on Breckinridge Street was in a panic, the sound of which soon spilled out into the street. Shrieks mingled with laughter that drifted on the air like dust from doily and dresser scarf shaken out the window.

"This can't be happening so quickly!" Georgia fairly breathed the words as her mother slipped her own wedding gown over her head.

"Oh, but it is, dear sister! Your Louis will be here tomorrow for your very own wedding, and that doesn't leave us with a lot of time to prepare," Jennie cried from across the room, a dust rag in one hand and lemon furniture wax in the other. She worked quickly to banish dust and dirt from every imaginable crevice.

Mary Wade was silent as she stood back to survey her oldest daughter, her firstborn, standing in the dress she herself had worn over two decades ago. She tried to focus on her daughter's face, which was beaming, rather than the dress itself, as the gown brought back too many memories, good and bad. And mostly she couldn't let go of the bad right now. She had been so happy when she first put on this gown, a gown that only needed a few tweaks to make it suitable for today's fashion.

And no matter how much she fought it, her eyes left the sanctuary of her daughters face, drifting down towards the dove grey satin billowing like a cloud at her feet. The memories, bittersweet, came unbidden, staccato-fashion, as she refused to give any of them undo attention. She saw her husband, John, standing proud, young and handsome beside her, his face full of hope and promise. Then came the children, happy days all, except for tiny Martha, who didn't make it to her first birthday. She saw John in their first house on Baltimore Street, a house much like the one they were living in now, with bedrooms upstairs, and the lower half divided between living quarters and tailor shop. John was good with a needle, if nothing else. He taught the girls and would have gone on to teach young John as well, but the stories were starting by then. The memories picked up speed now, too painful to be worth even a momentary glance. All except one, one memory that stood out from all the rest. One memory that had told her enough was enough, that her world would never be good, perfect, true, or hopeful again. John had supposedly "found" a wallet full of money on the street, and decided to keep it. And it wasn't even the keeping of the wallet that bothered her most, it was what he did with the wallet full of money. He took it and left, left her and the children behind, while he ran off to Washington City. He was arrested and thrown into prison, and the Wade family had been the talk of the town ever since. That was almost a dozen years ago now, a dozen years of scrimping and saving, sewing her own fingers into arthritic, twisted members to keep food on the table and this roof over their heads. It had been a hard life, and all of it leading up to this very moment.

The hopeful, carefree image of herself in this dress with John standing possessively beside her faded swiftly away, locked up tight within her heart, to be looked at again, perhaps, on some other dreamy day.

"Mama, are you crying?" Harry was sitting in the corner, out of the way, doing his best to polish a silver tray on loan from Maria Comfort, Georgia's best friend.

"Of, course not! All of this dust that your sister is raising is getting to my eyes, is all." The fact that the child noticed at all brought a fresh, unbidden run of tears that Mary Wade quickly dispatched with the corner of her apron.

"Mama, I know there is a poem about the color of a woman's wedding dress meaning something special, but I don't remember how it goes. Can you recite it for us, especially about the grey in George's dress." This was from Jennie, who hoped to get her mother thinking less of the past, or from dwelling on the future, and to focus more on the moment at hand. She, too, had noticed the tears, but was past the age of bringing it to anyone's attention. God bless the heart and eyes of a child!

"Oh, yes, please tell us all," chimed in Georgia.

"Well, let me see. How did that go? I know that the grey is for travel because I found it amusing that we left York, where your Pa and I were married, and moved to Gettysburg right afterwards. As for the rest of it, let's see, white means chosen right; blue, love will be true. Oh, yes, it's coming back to me now! Yellow, ashamed of her fellow; red, wish herself dead." This brought gasps and then peals of laughter from everyone in the room, including Mary Wade. "Well, I don't make this stuff up, you know. Let's see, there's also, black, wish herself back; pink, of you he'll always think; and green, ashamed to be seen." Her composure back under control, Mary stepped back from the dress she had been hemming to admire her daughter and all her youthful radiance. Taking her hands, she forced Georgia into a gentle swirl, the better to get an overall view.

"It's beautiful Georgia, you're positively radiant," Mary said, finally releasing her daughter's hands.

"Yes, George, it's absolutely beautiful! I've never seen a prettier bride," added Jennie. "Mama, isn't there a verse about the day of the week when a wedding takes place? Can you tell us all that one, too?"

"Oh, my, you're certainly putting me to the test today, aren't you? Let's see, I think I know that one better. It goes, Marry on Monday for health, Tuesday for wealth, Wednesday is the best day of all, Thursday for crosses, Friday for losses, and Saturday for no luck at all."

"What about Sunday, Mama," asked Harry, suddenly intrigued once more.

"Silly boy, no one gets married on a Sunday. And keep on polishing that tray. Don't think that listening to verses is going to get you out of a fair days' work," chided his mother.

"Well, I may not be getting married on Wednesday, which is the best day of all," giggled Georgia, "but at least I'm not getting married on Thursday or Friday. Not that I believe in all of that nonsense, of course, because I don't, but why tempt fate with crosses or losses when there's a war going on, right?"

Jennie nodded her head in agreement, then leaned out the window to shake the dust rag one more time. "You're right, George, Tuesday for wealth is much more practical."

Bright laughter filled the room as Georgia stepped closer to the full-length mirror in the corner, the better to see herself. It was the first real glimpse she had of her wedding dress, and she liked what she saw. Jennie clapped her hands in approval, and Harry and their mother quickly joined in.

Amidst the clapping and laughter, Harry piped up. "I know why you're wearing a grey dress for travel Georgia. It's not because you're the one doing the traveling, Louis is. Remember, he only has a couple days and he has to go back to the army."

Georgia let the grey satin folds of her skirt filter slowly through her fingers. The material drifted downward, like the smiles on all of their faces.

My Dearest Jack,

Well, our George is now a married woman. She and Louis McClellan are now a wedded couple. We tease Louis about his famous last name all the time, and he takes it in good stride. George, on the other hand, doesn't find it quite as amusing, her new name being George McClellan, and all. I promised not to tease her about it any more, but it still brings a smile to my face whenever I think about it.

Let me tell you about her wedding, because it brings a smile to my face when I think of it, too, and anything that brings a smile to my face during this dark period of war is something to be cherished indeed. It was a beautiful wedding! Grandma Filby came over early in the morning, and we all walked together to St. James Lutheran Church. We picked up Maria and Henry Comfort along the way, and several other friends joined in the procession, too. We were quite the joyful group when we met up with Louis's family at the church.

The wedding went off without a hitch, and George was beautiful in the grey dress that Mama wore at her own wedding to Papa over twenty years ago. But poor Mama, her eyes glistened with tears most of the day, and it was hard to tell by looking at her whether they were tears of joy or dreadful past memories. Mostly, I think she was just happy for George and that she had found a wonderful man to share her life with.

We had the traditional wedding breakfast at our house, after the service, and I don't have to tell you how crowded that house was! The Pierce's (the one's our brother Samuel works for) provided a large ham as a wedding gift, and Grandma Filby made the wedding cake as a gift. We had muffins, biscuits, sweetbreads, apple butter, honey, fried cakes, and I don't know what else. Everyone seemed satisfied with the bountiful table, and I don't think anyone walked away hungry. I found it amazing that, even amidst this war we could find amusement. We made patriotic cockades for the wedding guests, which in a way was a constant reminder of the war, but only seemed to want us to rise above the occasion and revel in having a good time. The latest tax on coffee, tea, and sugar were upsetting, but we substituted honey for the sugar, and added more water to the coffee and tea to make it stretch farther. As everyone is dong it in their own homes, no one seemed to mind we did it on this festive occasion as well. By early afternoon George and Louis were able to sneak away, as Louis had a surprise waiting for George. Grandma Filby had told him about a divided house that was for rent almost across the street from her place on the edge of town. Do you remember where she lives, on the south end of town near the Baltimore Pike? Well, that is where Louis rented a home for George and himself. It is a cute little place, and George says that I am not to be a stranger there.

On a sadder note, we are still hearing about a terrible battle that took place in Tennessee last week. It was near a place called Pittsburg Landing, but some of the papers are calling it The Battle of Shilo, after a church that stood nearby. It was a horrible battle, worse even than Bull Run! Every day the paper lists more names of dead and wounded soldiers. I think they said over ten thousand Union soldiers died there. I simply cannot imagine witnessing such a battle. How awful for those people who had to witness such a thing. I am ashamed to admit my selfishness, but I am glad you were not any where near that battle. God save us from such a day!

Tomorrow Mrs. Brinkerhoff will be bringing her young son, Isaac, over for me to watch. Do you remember that I said he was a crippled boy whose mother couldn't watch him when she went to work during the week? I met him for a few minutes last week, just to introduce myself, and found him a delightful little boy. I think he and Harry will get along just fine. He is only five years old, so not much younger than Harry, who is seven now. My hope is that the two of them can play together, allowing me more time to get my own work done. Perhaps you should say a prayer for me about that! At any rate, I know Mama will appreciate the extra income Mrs. Brinkerhoff will be paying me for this task.

Well, I think I have rambled on long enough. Do you ever get tired of my long missives? I know I do not get tired of reading yours. I treasure each one, reading them over and over until they almost fall apart at the crease. Perhaps you should send me more to replace those that have fallen apart. Promise me you will work on that Jack! I miss you terribly, and wish you could come home, even for a few days, like Louis did for George. Promise me you will work on that, too! Until then, I leave you with a prayer on my lips and the love in my heart.

Your dearest friend,

Jennie

May 21, 1862

Camp Buehler
Lutherville, Maryland

My Dear Jennie,

As you can see by the date on this letter, today is your birthday. I wanted to write sooner, but we are about to receive marching orders, to go where I do not know. There is talk that we might finally get to "see the elephant," but I hope that is not so. I do not fear battle, but neither do I wish to seek it out. I, too, have read the newspaper accounts on the battle that took place in Tennessee, and it was enough to make me appreciate the fact I was in Maryland, far from that act of carnage. But I am sure my time will come when I will be forced to raise my musket in defense of my country, just like the boys over there did, and I plan to be ready. God's will be done!

Life in camp is so dull sometimes. I think that is why some of the others look forward to battle. I much prefer a diversion of another sort. For most of us the best part of the day is mail call, and I always look forward to a letter from home or from you.

I was so glad to hear the report of George's fine wedding celebration. I am glad that Louis was able to get away, if only for a few days. I do not know how he managed it though, because I do not see men from this unit getting time off to go home on leave. I want to see you as much as I think you want to see me though, so I will keep on trying.

I was sorry to hear that the war is affecting things at home, like the new tax on tea and coffee. But if that is all that is affected, then that will surely count as a blessing. We usually have plenty of coffee to drink, but that is all that is palatable. The beef, when we get it, is usually quite stringy and tough. Mostly we make stew from it, for to eat it fried in a pan or cooked on a spit would be quite impossible. The hardtack, which is forced on us everyday, must be consumed in the same fashion, either dunked in our coffee or dropped into the stew. Some of the boys have developed a fashion of soaking the hardtack in coffee first, then frying it up in bacon grease. I think they call it skilleegallee, but there are so many different names for the stuff that I think some just make it up as they go along. Whatever name you want to call it, it still tastes the same, and that is awful! Which reminds me of another favorite pastime for us. We sit around at night, usually just before the evening meal, and talk about what we would really like to be looking forward to. We speak of dishes of roast chicken, good beef, pork roasts, fresh vegetables, not the desiccated vegetables they serve us around here. We would also love a nice piece of pie or cake, some fresh bread or biscuits. Some of the boys have actually received such delectables, but they are usually not in the best of shape by the time they arrive here. Also, there are instances where the goods don't arrive to the intended soldier, but land in someone else's hands instead. They call it being intercepted, but we all know what that means.

When next you write (and I hope it is soon) you must tell me all about your day today, what you did, and if you did anything special. You deserve a special day, and if I were there I would make it special indeed. Let's see, what would we do? I think we would take a walk in the evening, after supper, maybe out to that meadow by the spring on Culp's Hill. Do you remember the place? Wesley showed it to us, and the three of us used to have such fun there. Remember the time my brother Daniel came along and found that old log that the bees had decided to call home? To this day I'm not sure if he was brave or just stupid, sticking his hand into that thing and coming out with all of that honey. It sure tasted good though, and there was plenty to go around. Poor Wesley though, I never saw him run so fast! I sure could go for some of that honey now. I miss the taste of it, I miss my youthful friend, and I miss you, too. Let me hear from you soon, and tell me all the news of home.

Your affectionate friend,
Jack

Jennie softly closed her Bible and set it on the dresser near her bed. Her daily devotional complete, she mulled over Jesus' command to "love thy enemy" amidst the atrocities of this Civil War that surrounded them every day. It occurred to her that Jesus didn't know what He was asking, but then smiled at the absurdity of her own thought. Of course He knew! Until He came to save us we were all His enemies, and yet He loved us enough to be born into this sinful world, live among us, and allow Himself to be killed for our sake. It was absolutely the supreme act of showing how to treat ones enemies.

The sudden sound of raised, excited voices raced up the stairs from the kitchen below and she hurried to her feet. The horrid news about the latest battle, this time in nearby Maryland, had everyone on edge. Jennie fairly held her breath as she dashed down the stairs, expecting the worse. Rounding the corner into the kitchen, her eyes took in the room in one swift glance. Pots and pans hung neatly from pegs on the wall, and she noted that Harry had already deposited a supply of wood in the box near the wrought iron stove. Water hissed from the coffee pot atop the stove, and the fragrant aroma of baking biscuits assailed her nostrils. Her mother, eyes widen in shock, stood with her back to the screen door, one hand over her mouth, and the other holding her stomach as if she had just received an unexpected punch. Jennie followed her mother's gaze to the kitchen table where Georgia sat, hands folded neatly in her lap, tears ready to spill from her eyes, and a tremulous sort of smile toying with the corners of her mouth. Jennies own hand flew to her throat. She didn't know what the news was yet, but the fact that her sister was here now, this early in the morning, could not be taken as a good sign. It had to be Louis, she reasoned. Something bad must have happened to Louis, because if it was anyone else, well, then surely she, Jennie, would have been the first to know over Georgia, since Georgia doesn't even live in the household any more.

"What is it," Jennie whispered into the silence, afraid to even hear the answer. Mother and older daughter continued staring at each other as if alone in the room. Jennie ventured again, louder this time. "What's wrong? "

Finally, Georgia broke the stare down, turning her gaze to her sister. "Well, it seems Louis and I are going to have a baby." At that her smile grew wider, the stillness in the room was broken, and all three women screamed and laughed out loud. Jennie dashed to where her sister sat, beating her mother by mere inches. The three women laughed and embraced, nearly knocking Georgia right out of her chair. Instantly the once quiet room was filled with noise, as question followed question before answers could be given.

"How long have you known?"

"When is the baby due?"

"Does Louis know yet?"

Mary Wade sat down heavily in a nearby chair, dabbing at her eyes with the hem of her apron. Smiles remained on all of their faces, and finally Georgia regained her voice. "To answer your questions, yes, Louis does know. That is what took me so long to share the news with all of you. I wanted him to hear about it first, and once I got a letter back from him, saying how thrilled he was to learn of his pending fatherhood, well, then it was safe to share the news with the rest of my family. So, here I am. Our baby should come some time in late June, which is a good time, I think. Don't you, mother?"

"It's perfect, dear. The baby will be born before the worst of the hot summer days take hold. It's never pleasant to have to carry a baby through the heat of the summer, like I did with Samuel. He was the worst! But, say, wouldn't it be interesting if you had this little one on your own birthday? July 4th isn't that far removed from the end of June?"

Georgia wrinkled her nose and shook her head slightly. "Yes, that would be interesting, but I would prefer our baby to have his own special day and not have to share it with his mother."

"His? You're already claiming to have a son?" Jennie giggled at the absurdness of knowing what a baby was before it was born, and the other's joined in at the notion.

Georgia, who couldn't seem to stop smiling, giggled aloud. "No, silly, but when I told Louis the news he immediately made mention that having a son would be nice. I'm sure he would appreciate a daughter just as much, but you know how men are regarding sons."

"Yes, indeed," agreed their mother. "I remember well how your father's eyes shown when your grandmother walked into the room with your brother John in her arms. He screamed in such excitement that I believe everyone in town knew that John had arrived." Mary Wade giggled softly in remembrance, while Georgia, and particularly Jennie, grew very quiet. The very mention of their father brought an instant chill into the room. Jennie was too young to remember all of the details of her father's fall from grace, but at the tender age of eight she vividly recalled the day two sheriff deputies came to take him away, and her father stepped out of the house for the last time. Her mother cried for months, or so it seemed, and for years afterwards every time her family walked down the street people would turn the other way or whisper behind their hands. That, of course, was a long time ago, and people have allowed that awful stigma to fall from the Wade family like dead leaves in the fall. It was shortly after her father left, when her mother had finally regained her composure, that she had taught both Georgia and herself the tailoring trade. From that moment on, tailoring has been both the bane and pleasure of her very existence.

Mary Wade dabbed her eyes with her apron one final time, sensing that the quiet in the room was her own doing. "Listen to me, babbling on this way, and you sitting there without even a cup of tea in front of you yet. Jennie, did Harry bring us any water in from the well yet? Where is that child anyway?" Mary flew from her chair, a woman on a mission.

Jennie hugged her sister one last time, then retrieved cups and saucers from the shelf. Both knew that it would dawn on their mother, sooner or later, that Harry had brought in the water a long time ago, hence the hissing pot on the stove. But first she needed to work out some pent up emotions through mindless busy work. They watched silently, while mirth built slowly within, as their mother set the spoon holder on the table, replaced the cups and saucers on the shelf, reached in the drawer for the linen napkins, realized that the cups and saucers were missing and turned to retrieve them. Something made her look at the girls at that moment and she noted the barely concealed smiles on their faces. Alert now, she realized they had been watching her work through her emotions. The open smiles on their faces told her she had been forgiven for mentioning their father, but that they understood all too well the difficulty of keeping him forever banned from home, hearts, and memories.

"What's everyone laughing 'bout?" It was Harry, running into the room through the back door, which closed now with a bang. Still tucking in his shirt, it was obvious to all that he had just come from the necessary out back.

"You are soon to become an uncle, young man," Mary said, reaching for a towel to wipe his face and hands.

"I am? How?" Harry turned his puzzled face obediently towards his mother for further cleansing.

"George is going to have a baby next summer. What do you think about that?" Mary had banished all thoughts of her wayward husband now, wrapping herself instead in the supreme moment of acknowledgement – she was soon to be a grandmother!

"Next summer! We have to wait that long?"

Immediate laughter filled the room at Harry's expense. Mary tussled his hair before pulling him closer for a quick hug. Jennie finished setting the table for breakfast. Georgia's arrival and announcement had put them all off schedule.   Mrs. Brinkerhoff would be here soon with little Isaac, at which time things would really get busy.

Jennie glanced at her sister's face, enjoying the look of excitement and anticipation she saw there. She fairly glowed with hope and wonder! And as she leaned across the table with a platter of biscuits, Jennie felt the newest letter from Jack crinkle in her apron pocket, a gentle reminder that she, too, might one day experience those same emotions of pending motherhood.

At that moment there was a knock at the door. Jennie wiped her hands on her apron, all the while moving towards the door. She opened it to reveal Mrs. Brinkerhoff holding a sleepy-eyed little boy in her arms. "Good morning Mrs. Brinkerhoff," Jennie greeted.

"Good morning to you, Miss Wade."

Jennie stepped aside so the pair could enter the house. Isaac presented her with a shy smile, but his eyes darted through the room, searching for Harry. Isaac was a small, slight child with blonde curly hair that, upon first glance, was in much need of a combing. But further inspection made one wonder if that was at all possible, the curls being so tight as to defy any attempt at combing or brushing. Mrs. Brinkerhoff held tightly to Isaac, and he did the same, the love of mother and child clearly evident. Isaac was barefoot, as most boys this time of year, and his clothes showed much attention to repeated repair. Jennie's heart melted all over again, just like it did at her first introduction.

"Harry," she called, "your friend, Isaac, is here!"

Harry came on the run, squealing with delight at each step he took. Jennie accepted Isaac from his mother, who was torn between needing to leave for work and wanting to stay with her son. One more, quick kiss, one more tussle of curly hair, and

Mrs. Brinkerhoff slipped out the door. She breathed a soft "thank you," to Jennie and let the latch fall into place.

Jennie carried Isaac to a nest of blankets on the floor of the kitchen where he and Harry spent a good part of the day. Here they were both out of the way, but close enough for observation. Here they could play quietly, at least that was always the plan, and have full access to door and window should they want to look outside. The biggest blessing about the arrangement was the readiness with which Harry accepted that Isaac could not walk and no longer questioned that fact. Granted he and she had many conversations about Isaac's condition and how he was so special in God's eyes, unique in every way, but at least Harry had stopped asking for explanations in Isaac's presence now. They were the best of friends, and it did Jennie's heart good to watch the two of them getting along so famously.

Georgia rose and headed for the door. "I'm sorry I can't stay any longer but I have some errands to run before I have to be to Grandma's house. She wants some help with sorting out yard for socks for the soldiers."

"How so," questioned Mrs. Wade.

"It seems that someone from church passed recently, leaving several baskets full of yarn that the family doesn't want under foot any longer. Rather than toss it into the garbage heap they offered it to Grandma to sort through and make some sense of the mess. I guess 'mess' is a good word for it, too, the way Grandma talked about it. Some of it is rolled neatly into balls, but most of it is simply tossed into the basket willy-nilly. A lot of it is hopelessly tangled, with pieces of scrap material mixed in for good measure, and it is caught up in the sides of the straw basket as well. I'm sure there will be plenty that we won't be able to use at all, at least not for socks or mittens, but if we can salvage even a little bit it will be a true blessing for our soldiers in arms."

"Well, it seems you do have your work cut out for you today, dear. Give my mother a hug for me, will you? And tell her I will try and get down there and help out myself sometime soon, though it sounds like you might have things under control right nicely."

Jennie tossed her sister a smile and a wave good-bye before heading for the tailor shop where a days worth of work awaited her, too. Her mother entered the room right behind her, moving towards the sewing machine in the corner. "I hate the thought of putting this horrid trim on such lovely fabric, but Mrs. Hoffmann is positively smitten by it and insists it is the perfect color for her," Mrs. Wade commented. The chair scraped noisily across the bare wood floor as she dragged it closer to the machine. "What do you think, Jennie, do you think this is appropriate trim for such a dress and fabric?"

"Jennie glanced in her mother's direction, eyeing the dark navy blue satin dress fabric and the teal blue rouching her mother held up for inspection. "Well, I agree it might have a bit too much green in it to do justice for the dress. But you're right about Mrs. Hoffmann being smitten with it. I thought I heard her say she ordered it special all the way from New York City, and it didn't come cheap either. Sometimes Mama, as you well know, we simply have to do whatever the customer wants and keep our mouths closed in the bargain."

Mrs. Wade was on the verge of saying something more when a sudden crash from the other room brought Jennie to her feet in a flash. "Harry! Is everything all right in there," she asked on the run.

She entered the room to find Harry hovering over a puddle of water in the middle of the kitchen floor. "Isaac wanted to know what it was like to go fishing, and I was going to this here kettle like it was a pond. But somehow it got too full."

"Somehow it got too full," Jennie repeated, mimicking her brother, while hurrying to the rag box at the same time. Isaac sat in the corner with a look on his face that said he hoped the floor would just open up and swallow him whole, while Harry was doing more sloshing of the water than mopping. She knew she couldn't stay angry with them for long. It had been an honest, though childish accident after all. Taking the rag from Harry's hand, she bid him pick up the kettle and replace it on the stove instead. Before she was half finished with the puddle on the floor she heard her mother calling from the tailor shop. Her voice sounded urgent. "Jennie! Can you help me with this blasted sewing machine! It is eating Mrs. Hoffmann's dress fabric and I can't get it to release!"

Jennie, still on her knees in the middle of the kitchen floor, glanced heavenward and blew a wayward length of long brown hair from across her face. Rising to her feet, hands on hips, she turned from one disaster to the next and mumbled under her breath. "Thus begins another day in the Wade household."

Gettysburg
Sept. 22, 1862

My Dearest Jack,

I have so much to tell you, I scarce know where to begin. Once more our ears were assaulted by the screaming of the newsboy on the corner. Another terrible battle, probably the worst ever, has taken place, this time on Maryland soil. That is far too close to home! Like most everyone else in town, I ran to the corner, over on Baltimore Street, to read through the list of names, and believe me, it was a long list. It is a very odd sensation to be glancing through a list of names "searching" for that one particular one, and praying you don't find it. Then, when you get to the end of the list, you have to wonder if the list was complete, and whether there will be another list tomorrow. It is enough to break a woman's heart!

Where are you Jack? The last letter I received from you said you were getting ready to march, but you didn't say where. I ran into your mother down at Fahnestock's the other day and she said she hadn't heard from you in over a week. (She's upset about that, by the way.) But in her last letter from you she, too, said you had mentioned something about breaking camp and going on the march. Not knowing where you are causes us all manner of distress, and it is that not knowing that makes us run when the newsboy begins his hawking. I don't mean to berate you, I really don't, it's just that I don't know what I'd do if something happened to you. I wish that you would tell me your marching orders are having you march right back to Gettysburg. Wouldn't that be something?

Your sister, Annie, was with your mother when we met. She is growing into quite the young lady. She proudly told me that she was six and a half years old now, and quite eager to quit school in order to do something for her Papa and brothers that are away fighting in the war. Apparently some of the neighborhood boys have told her that all Rebels are worthy of only one thing, and that is death. I asked her what she thought her brother or Papa should do if they ran into Wesley Culp, and she said, "why, shoot him, of course." When I reminded her that Wesley was our friend, she simply said that he should have made better choices. My heart sank upon hearing her recital, and your mother didn't seem to like it very much either. She bid me a hasty good day and hustled your little sister away down the street.

But speaking of helping our beloved soldiers so far from home, did you know that a lot of women have taken to knitting socks, mittens and scarves during church service now? The Pastor's in several local churches have heard that churches in other nearby towns, like Carlisle and Chambersburg, have taken up the practice, so we are joining in as well. He jokingly said that he did not want to see sewing machines set up in the isles, but anything we can do to further help our boys without disrupting the flow of the service is fine with him. He prefers, however, that we do our work for the good of all the soldiers and not just our own family members. There is a box near the entryway where our finished items are to be placed, and when the box is filled he will see that the Christian Commission or Sanitary Commission gets the items into the right hands. I think that is a fine idea, though I would much rather be doing all of my knitting for you only. I will pretend that while I am working on mittens that they are for your hands only, and then make special ones for you while I am at home.

Mama is doing more than knitting socks for the soldiers now, and so am I. While she is knitting booties, I am working on a baby quilt in the evenings. Guess who these items are for. If you said George, you would be right. She and Louis are expecting a little visitor next summer, isn't that wonderful? Needless to say, we are all very excited around here!

Harry and Isaac, the little boy I watch during the week

(remember, I told you about him) are both looking forward to having another playmate, not realizing that it will be awhile before any child born next summer will be capable of playing with them. By then they will both be that much older and not want the child to be around them. As for me, I can't wait to hold that little baby in my arms!

So, you see, things have been quite exciting here in Gettysburg. But not as exciting as it would be if I knew you were coming home. Have you found out if you can get a leave yet, Jack? It would be wonderful to see you again, if only for a little while. I miss you so! I carry your daguerreotype with me always, but it would be nice to see the real thing for a change. Please take care of yourself for me and know that there is one place where you are always safe - deep within my heart!

Your most devoted friend,
Jennie

October 12, 1862
Buckhanon, Upshure County Virginia

Dearest Jennie,

Thank you for your latest letter. It is always wonderful to hear from you and learn that you are doing as well as can be expected during this time of war. It is sad that it doesn't touch the soldier only, but has such long reaching affects. I look forward greatly to receiving the mittens or scarf or whatever else it is you are making for me, especially as the weather is turning colder now, and most especially at night.

As you can see from the post on this letter, we have moved since the last time I wrote. We have moved farther into Virginia now, the farthest we have gone so far, but I don't expect that we will be here too much longer. There is already talk about moving on, some say to Stanton, but I'm not sure. Right now we are camped near the prettiest little village I think Virginia has to offer. It is really first rate. I wish you could see it, I think you would agree.

Thank you for telling me about meeting Ma and Annie. Ma writes often, of course, but it is always good to hear about home from another source. I don't know why, but it makes everything seem alive and real somehow. That Annie of mine sure is something, isn't she? Ma told me pretty much the same story, about her talking about Wesley that way, but I think it's because she doesn't really know who Wesley is. If I remember right, Annie was born the month after Wesley left town with Hoffman's carriage company. Had we only known where that decision would have led him, I know I would have tried harder to talk him out of going. As it is, we hardly ever talk about Wesley, especially while his brother William is around. It is the saddest thing to realize that brother is fighting against brother in this fashion. Worse, still, to think what would happen if they should actually meet in battle. What would be the outcome, I wonder.

But amidst all this talk of battle and war there comes the news about an expected baby. What good news for you, George, and your whole family. Life goes on, right? What about Louis, where is he these days? I am still surrounded by our childhood friends, William Ziegler, William Holtzworth, William Culp, and my brother Charles, so at least I have familiar faces to keep me company. But there is another whose face I long to see even more. Can you guess whose face that might be?

I have to tell you about another new dish we have become accustomed to. It is called ramrod bread and is really quite good. I don't remember who cane up with the idea, but we saw a fellow do it one time, and before you know it, it spreads through camp like the measles. What we do is make a dough from flour, water and some sugar, then wrap it around a stick or a ramrod, and slowly bake it over the fire. It would taste better with some apple butter, honey or sweet butter, but as we usually don't have those available, we simply eat it plain, and right off the stick. It doesn't compare to what we would get back home, but then nothing has since I joined up. Sometimes that's all we do is grumble about the food, the lack of sleep and the horrid sleeping conditions, the constant drilling and marching, and the lack of privacy we've all had to get used to. Many are the night's we simply sleep under the stars, and those night's can sometimes be just fine, but when it's raining it is much harder to get a good night's sleep. We have gum blankets to crawl under when it's raining, but if it rains real hard then little streams of water always find their way under. It is amazing what the human body can endure or get used to, and I pray you never have to suffer it.

Our ranks have thinned out quite a bit since I first signed up, but the thinning isn't from battle, skirmishing, or any other kind of fighting. No, our dwindling numbers come from the many illnesses that seem to attack faster than the Rebels can find us. Dysentery is the worse, but there are several that have come down with measles and several different kinds of fevers. I, myself, just got over a really bad cold, and am very thankful that it didn't develop into pneumonia. I know I wouldn't have suffered as much and would have gotten over it faster if I had been able to devour some of my mother's chicken soup, or any decent soup, but none was to be found anywhere around here. I can't remember the last time I ate chicken in any form!

You keep asking me to get a furlough and I want you to know that I would if I could. I would like nothing better than to come home, if even for a short time, but it is impossible right now. They are very stingy with furloughs right now and I don't see that changing any time soon. I have signed on to see this war to the end, and it might take me that long before I get to see you or home again. Mother keeps asking me to apply for a furlough as well, which gets me to wondering if the two of you aren't in cahoots with each other. Believe me when I say no one wants a furlough more than myself, and if there is any possibility of getting one, I will. There, does that ease your mind any?

Well, it is getting late and the fire is dying down such that I can barely see to write any more. I will say good night for now and *will try and write more later, but I don't know when that will be as we have received marching orders and will be breaking camp real soon. Give my best to your family, and to George and her new baby. Let me hear from you soon. You can still reach me at this post. They will forward the mail to our new camp and I will let you know what the new post is at that time. Take care of yourself Jennie!*

Your truest and most devoted friend,
Jack

"I love this time of day," offered Mary Wade, sighing contentedly. She and Jennie were sitting opposite each other in the front room set aside as their tailor shop, each busy with a sewing project. Jennie was sewing trim on a chemise, while her mother hemmed a pair of trousers for a customer.

"How so," asked Jennie, her fingers moving deftly across the white fabric, her eyes never leaving their objective.

"Well, it's so quiet and peaceful right now. That late afternoon sun through the window is good for my eyesight, and I love the warmth of the sun on my hands." She nodded towards the boys, Harry and Isaac, sitting on the floor in the corner where they had been playing, now with backs against the wall, lost in slumber. "And they have finally settled down from their awful war games. Don't get me wrong, now, because I adore that they get along so, but there is so much talk of war any more. It creeps into every aspect of our lives, and I find it so tiring any more.

The latest news from the front is on everyone's lips, it affects the prices at market, we pray about it in church, and now it is even showing up in ladies fashion, what with the military stripes and buttons and all. And if that's not enough, the children want to play it under our very noses. It's enough to make the stoutest heart tremble!"

"I know what you mean, Mama. I still can't get used to bringing a sewing basket to church on Sunday's, but I almost feel out of place if I'm not sewing or knitting something for the boys." Jennie bit the thread from the final stitch, tossed the finished chemise across a nearby chair and stretched her back muscles, kneading them with her hands at the same time. "Would you care for a cup of tea Mama? I believe I'll put the pot on."

Her sentence was barely finished when her brother, John, dashed into the room. He paused only a moment to catch his breath, and in that instant the slam of the screen door finally caught up with him. "Mama, did you hear? Did you hear the news?"

Jennie's hand flew to her throat, her brother's sudden and loud appearance catching her off guard, but Mary Wade, used to her son's theatrics, took it more in stride.

"Sweetie, we haven't heard anything but the singing of birds through the window and the soft snoring of two little boys until you burst through that door like a bull out of a pen and scared the poor things near half to death. Now, what is this ruckus all about, and pray, tell me that you wiped those big feet of yours before you came running into this house!"

"No, Mama, I forgot. But wait til you hear! The Rebels are in Chambersburg! They say it's General Stuart with over a thousand men, and he's burning and killing everything in sight! Now can I join the army?"

"Chambersburg? But that's only a days ride away," exclaimed their mother. Her sewing went forgotten for the time being, as her son had her full attention now.

The two boys, silent in the corner, were both wide awake now. It was hard to determine whether their startled looks were from a rude awakening or the frightening news of enemy soldiers so close to home. Harry rubbed a small fist to his eye, the better to see and think more clearly. "Mama, what are we going to do?"

"Hush, child, I have to think!" Harry knew from the tone in his mother's voice that she wasn't really mad at him, yet the sense of urgency brought quiet all the same.

Rising to her feet, Mrs. Wade disentangled herself from the trousers in her lap and moved towards the kitchen. The kitchen, the main room in the house, the room where most important decisions were made, the room where thinking would be more clear.

"Mama, what about the army? Can I join up now?" John hadn't moved from his position in the doorway, only shifting his attention from the sewing room to kitchen.

"John, we have been over this before. You're too young, and I need you here at home. Those Rebels aren't going to make it as far as Gettysburg, our own soldiers won't allow it. Now I told you we'd talk about it more when you turned seventeen, did I not, and you still have five more months until that will be a reality."

"But..."

"Meanwhile, why don't we try and see what's really going on."

"But, Mama, can't I at least join the militia? If those Rebels make it through Chambersburg they're bound to head straight for Gettysburg, and I can do more for my family with a musket in my hand than hiding behind women's skirts!"

"John, please! Not right now, and let that be the end of it!"

The small battle inside the house paled in comparison to the noise level rising from the street outside. Jennie, closest to the door, flung it open and stepped out onto the porch. People were gathering on the corners of both Baltimore and Washington Streets, mingling in small groups that were growing by the second. Their voices rose by each additional member, everyone trying to gain attention and out shout his neighbor. Without a second thought, she shouted. "I'll be right back," and dashed out onto the road towards Baltimore Street. The prettily singing birds and the warmth of the sunshine her mother had spoken of earlier were all but forgotten as Jennie made her way to the throng on the corner. She didn't try to speak. It would have been pointless anyway, as her voice would have been swallowed up by the ever growing cacophony of men and women's voices all bent on the same thing, seeking information. So impromptu was the gathering that neither Jennie, nor several of the other women in the crowd even bothered to put on bonnets. Most of the faces in the still growing crowd were familiar to Jennie. There was Maria Comfort, who lived just down the street; Mr. Pierce, from the butcher shop where her brother, Samuel, lived and apprenticed; Jack's mother, looking frantic, had just arrived; and she noticed that her brother, John, had managed to get away from the house and their own mother again. The poor newsboy, his face near panic, must have felt overwhelmed by all of the shouting and attention he was receiving. Several times she noticed that he handed out a paper without benefit of payment. Mr. Schultz, a member of their church, had a paper in his hand, and as he was the nearest person with such a treasure, she moved in his direction.

"Please, Mr. Schultz, can you tell me what it says?" Jennie raised her voice to be heard over the crowd. She was rewarded with a quick, acknowledging smile, and then Mr. Schultz wiggled his way to the back of the crowd for a little elbowroom.

"Well, let's see..." Mr. Schultz folded the paper in order to afford a better view of the article that had captured everyone's attention.

"Are there really over a thousand Rebel soldiers heading

this way?"

Mr. Schultz' thick German accent seemed stronger as he struggled to read the article out loud. "Vell, yah, it says there were about 1,800 enemy soldiers under General JEB Stuart that ran into Chambersburg around 7:00PM last night."

"Eighteen hundred," someone exclaimed!

"But it was raining real hard then, if I remember right."

"Yah, it was raining hard," Mr. Schultz commented, and then continued with the article. "They were met by several of the town officials, a Judge Kimmell and a Col. McClure, who managed to send a telegram to Governor Curtain just before the telegraph wires were cut."

"Oh, my, they cut the wires?"

"Yah, yah, the wires were cut all right. And then they started appropriating, that's the word they used, appropriating all of the town's rifles and ammunition, and clothing, and just about everything else they could carry. What they couldn't carry away with them, they destroyed."

"They destroyed the towns goods?" The same woman who had a penchant for echoing Mr. Schultz's words seemed close to panic. She reached for a hanky in her apron pocket while her husband did his best to shush her.

"But, was anyone killed," someone asked.

"No, it does not say anything about them killing anyone, Praise God."

Jennie listened as Mr. Schultz shared some more of the article with her and the others who had gathered around. It was a terrifying article full of burning buildings, looted stores, and frightened citizens.

The crowd gathering in the street had grown less rowdy as information was imparted and shared. Though none of the news was good, there was a sense of safety in numbers, and they commiserated with their friends and family members from the nearby town. One woman shrieked when she heard the news, screaming about her daughter and son-in-law that operated a mercantile in Chambersburg. Several women surrounded her, offering words of encouragement and the strength of friendly arms to support her. Others, like many of the men in the crowd, voiced violent opinions.

"Wait til our soldiers get there!"

"Those Rebels will get a what for then, believe me!"

"They're probably half way through Dixie even now!"

"I can't believe the cowards, cuz that's what they are, have attacked a town full of defenseless women and children!"

Jennie absorbed the words of bravado, gaining a sense of calm. Realizing that she had worked her apron into a worried ball, she let it fall from her hands, straightening it across her long skirt. Glancing over the crowd she noted her brother John had located a small circle of friends. Their faces were serious as they gesticulated wildly, slamming fist into open palm, or slapping cap against thigh. She couldn't hear their words, but she suspected they were discussing wasted opportunities of chasing Rebels that had dared come so close to home.

"There's more," Mr. Schultz called out, and the nearby crowd quieted, waiting to hear what else he had to say. "The Rebels have been to Cashtown as well."

"Cashtown! But that's only eight miles away," someone shouted.

Instantly the crowd was in uproar again. John and his friends became more animated, and several women broke from the crowd, rushing to home and hearth, their skirts lifted halfway to their knees. It was almost more than a person could bear, knowing that the enemy was within eight miles of home!

Slowly Jennie inched her way through the crowd. For a brief moment her eyes locked on Jack's mother, standing on the outer edge of a crowd that was growing by the minute. Like most of the townspeople, Jack's mother seemed terror stricken. And when Jenny finally caught up with the woman, they gripped hands firmly, finding momentary strength in each other's weakness. Neither spoke, there was really no need. Bound together by the love of one man, their hearts beat for him now, and fear of self was forgotten. Jennie's free hand instinctively found its way into her apron pocket where Jack's picture and latest letter always lay. She knew most of the words by heart now, the letter reread so many times, and words of her next letter to him were already forming in her head.

A quick glance down Breckenridge Street revealed her mother standing on the front porch, hands kneading a hankie into a ball. She was staring in the direction of the crowd, obviously waiting for Jennie's return. Gently disengaging herself from Jack's mother, she gave the woman a tremulous smile. Then, wrapping her arms around her in a quick hug, she hurried off to her own mother to share the frightful news.

October 12, 1862
Gettysburg, Penn

My Dearest Jack,

I thought I would never get chores done or the house in order so that I could find time to write to you tonight. I have thought of nothing but you all day now. You will not believe what happened only a few days ago. It is most dreadful news! The Rebel army ventured into Pennsylvania all the way to Chambersburg, where they burned most of the town, stole whatever they could carry away, and struck fear into the hearts of citizens for miles around. There are even reports that they tramped through Cashtown on their way back south. Their famous General Jeb Stuart is said to be the one who led them here. They say he was mostly looking for supplies, but I also think he was trying to send a message to we Union folk about what an army they are to reckon with. And I must say, if fear is what they were trying to spread, then they succeded! Gettysburg was in an absolute uproar! With Cashtown being only eight miles away, we certainly realized just how vulnerable we are as a tiny village.

But the Rebel army is gone now, back deep into their southland. I think we can breathe a little bit easier now just knowing that. Yet, I still wonder where you are, Jack. Are you safe? And I wonder what would happen if the Rebel army ever tried coming this far north again. All we have is a little militia force filled with old men, store clerks, and boys too young to enlist in the army yet, to protect us. It would be comforting to know that you would march to our rescue. But then, were I to see you again, I know that I would wrap my arms around you and never let you go again. I think that could cause a whole different set of problems, don't you?

This is truly a scary time that we live in, Jack. We hear about the battles being fought in far off places, we see the rising cost of goods, and read about the threat of shortages, but never did I think the war would ever get closer than that. And now it was here, practically on our doorstep! I wonder, too, about Wesley, our dear old friend. Do you think he might have been part of that invading force? I wonder what the townspeople would do if he were to show up wearing the grey uniform. Would they look on him in fear, or disgust, or maybe disdain. Or would they remember him as the sweet little boy who used to roam these very streets with us, and whose own parents still live just down the street from here. I simply can't imagine. As for me, I think I would embrace him like in days of old. And you would have nothing to be jealous of, nothing to fear, for you know how close we three were, and where my true heart lies.

Though the hour is late, I can still hear the townspeople meandering in the street, their voices raised in protest and fear of the Rebel invasion I just told you about. I admit that I found no appetite for dinner, and my sewing suffered during the evening hours, but writing to you now seems to have lifted that burden of fear I carried around with me most of the day. Why is that, I wonder. I know there is nothing you can do about the situation, not even if they should return tomorrow. God forbid! But unburdening to you this way has left me with a sense of calm, and I know that after I say my prayers tonight and lay down to sleep, that sleep will indeed come, and I will wake tomorrow ready to face another day. I better, too, because I have a lot of sewing to make up for after the way I botched it this afternoon.

Well, my dear friend, I should say good night now. It is getting late and my candle is burning rather quickly. Wherever you are, I pray that you are safe and warm and lack for nothing. I'll tell you again, though I don't think I should have to remind you that you are in my prayers constantly. Please take care of yourself, Jack, and hurry home to me.

Your best and dearest friend,
Jennie

November 12, 1862
Shenandoah Valley

Dearest Jennie,

I was greatly distressed to hear about your near encounter with the Confederate army. I can certainly understand your fears and those of the whole town. I heard from mother as well, and she mentioned that several of the local stores were ready to pile their stuffs onto wagons and haul it to safety someplace else, though where they thought they would go with it is beyond me. Still, better to make the effort than lie down like a dog in the street and let them ride right over you! I am glad that the danger is passed now, and hopefully those Rebels will never again venture anywhere close to our beloved State and home town.

This letter is going to be a short one as I am very tired. We have been marching all over the countryside these past several weeks. We have been marching up hill and down, in the rain and in the bright sunshine until my feet are nearly worn right off! It seems we are never in one place long enough to get comfortable or even to get a proper rest. There was much grumbling, as that is all we are able to do about it, but otherwise our spirits are pretty high. That is until we heard about Chambersburg and how close the enemy got to home. There was much talk about desertion then, but I don't know anyone who actually left the ranks. I have to say, though, Heaven help those Rebels if they ever venture that close to my home and family again! By Golly, they will get the war they are after then!

It is hard to believe that I have been in the army for a year and a half already. I really didn't think the war would go on this long. I am not the only one who thinks this either, though I don't hear too many men saying they would change anything had they known. Most of them are very patriotic and say they would sign up again tomorrow, regardless of how long the war goes on. I am one of those men. Be aware that I know I am needed at home, too. But what kind of a man would I be if I let others march off and do what I am totally capable of doing myself? This is my country, the land of my birth, and my blood boils when I think of those who would tear it asunder. No! It must be preserved, for the family I have now, and the family I want to have in the future. You can understand that, right?

Well, I feel I have been on my soapbox long enough, I think. You can probably chalk it up to weariness in body and spirit. A soldier's life is a hard one, to be sure, and I think I have adapted as well as any man here. But we do get lonely, tired and hungry, and long for home. The weather is turning colder now, especially at night. We don't always have enough wood to keep a fire going all night long, so we tend to jealously guard what we do have. It's a hard plight though, as our Christian spirit always takes over when we see one of our fellow mates in need of a common essential, like firewood. The country we are marching through is very beautiful, as well. Most of the trees have long last lost their leaves, but even that cannot take away from the beauty of this place. The ground is very fertile, and the farms seem quite prosperous. We are constantly on the lookout for the enemy, though I think it would be sad to wage war on this ground. There is talk that we will soon be going into winter quarters, but I can't say that I am looking forward to that. Being in winter quarters can be very tiresome, with not much to do during the day to keep one occupied. It is during such times that men speak of home more fondly, and sometimes even act on thoughts of going home. You probably know what I am referring to – desertion. I can understand why a man might entertain such a notion, but I cannot condone acting upon it. I think running away from this fight, from comrades, from a country that needs every man it can get is tantamount to treason, and on a more personal level, the most selfish act a man could undertake. But, listen to me, climbing back onto my soapbox once more. I think hearing your news about the closeness of the enemy to our homes has affected me more than I imagined it would.

As you can see, I am quickly running out of writing paper, and I do not want to leave you with such sad words to read. Please know that, in spite of my grumblings, I am doing as well as can be expected. Thoughts of you keep me going, even when my limbs want to falter. When I am weary in body from marching long hours, I think how bad off this country would be if every soldier quit and went home when the urge came upon him. I think how quickly would our country be swallowed up by those who would do it harm, and I simply put one more foot in front of the other, with your face as my beacon. Dearest Jennie, stay brave, even if the enemy comes close. Know that I am out here doing whatever I can to keep them away from you and our home and that I will be back as quickly as I can. Until that day arrives, I remain...

Your most trusted and truest friend,
Jack

Christmas Day, and Harry sat at the kitchen table as patiently as any seven-year old can while waiting for dinner. Mrs. Wade poured thin gravy into a bowl, while Jennie sliced their bread thinly and wrapped it in a towel for warmth.

"Where is your brother John," Mrs. Wade asked the two of them.

"He walked down to get Samuel and should be back any moment, I expect," answered Jennie.

"Samuel is coming too?" Harry sat up straighter in his chair, excitement beaming on his face.

"Yes, and Georgia and your Grandma and Grandpa Filby, as well," added his mother. The mention of additional guests was brought up as a distraction to what Mrs. Wade knew was coming next. It was Harry's time worn question, and asked each time they sat down to a large family meal.

"Why doesn't Samuel live with us?" And there it was!

Mrs. Wade reached for another pan from its hook on the wall, and explained as patiently as possible to her young son again. "I've told you before, dear, your brother is old enough now to learn a trade. So when Mr. Pierce, at the butcher shop, offered to take Samuel in as an apprentice, why it was an answer to a prayer."

"But why?"

"Because Samuel would be getting an education that I would not be able to provide, and he didn't have to go faraway to get it."

"But what would he learn?"

"He'd learn how to be a butcher."

"But..."

"And it was one less mouth to feed. Or to listen to! Harry, why don't you go outside and see if you can spot your grandparents and Georgia coming down the street."

"This is going to be like a real party! I love Christmas! Is Isaac coming too?" Harry's excitement grew as he slipped off his chair and bounded for the door.

Jennie smiled at her younger brother's youthful exuberance. "No, Isaac is not coming today," she told him.

"Why not?" Harry whined, his enthusiasm for the day dampened slightly.

"Because it's Christmas, silly. His mother doesn't have to work, so he'll be spending the day with his own family. Don't you think he'd want to be with his own family on such a special day as Christmas?"

"I guess."

"Good! Now hurry on and see about Grandma, Grandpa, and Georgia."

"All right!" Harry snatched his coat from a peg by the door, and allowed it to slam behind him on his way out.

"Oh, how that child can go on!" Mrs. Wade continued to mash potatoes on the stove, happy now that she wasn't playing question and answer with her youngest any more. She groaned a playful groan when her oldest son came into the room.

John plopped down at a place at the table. "Is dinner almost ready?"

"Elbows off the table, please," Jennie remonstrated, rolling her eyes. She took a moment to stand back and eye the table. An extra plank had been placed in it, extending it another two feet. It would still be crowded, but it would suffice. A used-to-be white linen tablecloth hid the rough lumber beneath, making it appear almost elegant in the dimly lit room. Heavy clouds hid the sun, making the early afternoon seem more like early evening instead. But the room was cheerful and inviting. The cook stove had been going since early morning, making use of the fireplace unnecessary. The aroma of fresh bread, apple pie, and roasted leg of lamb filled every crevice of the house. It had been that way ever since they had returned from the Christmas Day service at church this morning.

The Wade family was not rich, never had been, but their home was pretty typical for a family celebrating the Christmas season. Pine boughs had been brought in to drape across the fireplace mantle, bringing the scent of outdoors inside. A small Christmas tree stood atop a table near the door that divided the living quarters of the house from the tailor shop. It was decorated with paper cutouts, cookies, popcorn, and spare bits of ribbon, all lovingly and eagerly prepared by Harry, Isaac and herself. It wasn't much, but it added greatly to the festivity of the occasion. And then there were the little gifts, one for each person in the household, set beneath the tree. Other families with bigger trees might place their gifts right on the branches of their trees, but the Wade family Christmas tree was too small a tree to support the weight of wrapped gifts of any size.

The house was quiet for the moment, with Harry off on his errand and, Isaac, his partner in crime at home with his own family. Samuel was not yet here, and John, with his eyes closed, seemed intent on devouring the Christmas meal through scent alone. Jennie eyed the tree one more time, its small pile of gifts more enticing than food for the moment. Quietly walking the few steps in its direction, she gingerly fingered the gifts, wondering which one might be hers. None of them had labels, so there was no way to know whose was whose. Only the giver of the gift would be able to recognize his or her creation, and that was just fine, unless you were of the curious nature and desperately wanted to know which one was yours.

"Jennie Wade! What are you doing at that Christmas tree?" Mrs. Wade entered the room to set another dish on the table, her loud reprimand scaring both Jennie and John at the same time. John jumped two feet off his chair, an act that made both women laugh out loud. Jennie stepped away from the Christmas tree, her cheeks red with mirth, as well as the blush of a girl caught in a childlike criminal act.

In that same instant the front door opened and in walked Georgia, Harry, Grandma and Grandpa. "Look who I found walking down the street," announced Grandpa as Samuel came in right behind.

"Merry Christmas," he cried, the greeting of which was

quickly picked up and passed around the room. It hovered in the air, mingling with the sweet aroma of baking bread and apple pie, and filling their hearts with the magic of it all.

Later that evening when everyone was full from their Christmas meal and the last dish had been put away, the family gathered in the living room. Mrs. Wade sat on the horsehair sofa between her parents, while Georgia claimed the wooden rocker. Harry and Samuel sat on the floor near the fireplace, and John had brought two kitchen chairs into the room for Jennie and himself.

"Thank you for a wonderful meal, Mama," Jennie began, a sentiment that was quickly picked up by everyone in the room.

"Don't thank me, you had as much a hand in it as I did, Jennie. And lets not forget to thank Samuel for bringing the leg of lamb in the first place. That was a wonderful gesture on Mr. Pierce's part. You be sure to thank him for us all tomorrow, son."

"I already did, Mama. But he said it was the least he could do on account of you allowing him to gain the best apprentice he could ever hope to find in this town."

Samuel would have gone on, but his tongue in cheek boasting was more than his older brother could stand. A pillow went sailing across the room, catching Samuel full in the face. Laughter quickly filled the room, and Harry took advantage of his brother's weakened state by jumping on him. Seconds later they were both locked in a wrestlers embrace, arms and legs flying in every direction, each trying to pin the other to the floor. But before things could get too far out of hand, especially being that close to the fireplace, Mrs. Wade loudly announced, "who's ready to open presents?"

Harry was off of his brother in an instant. "I am!"

"Good! But first comes the Christmas story. Jennie would you do the honors, dear?"

71

"Of course, Mama." Jennie reached down for the family Bible, which had already been placed near her chair in anticipation of this very moment. As she fingered through the well-worn pages, looking for the passages in Luke, John got up to place another log on the fire. When he was settled, Jennie cleared her throat and began to read. "From Luke, chapter two, beginning at verse one, "and it came to pass in those days, that there went out a decree from Caesar Augustus, that all of the world should be taxed. And this taxing was first made when Cyrenius was governor of Syria. And all went to be taxed, every one into his own city. And Joseph also went up from Galilee out of the city of Nazareth, into Judea, unto the city of David, which is called Bethlehem because he was of the house and lineage of David, to be taxed with Mary his espoused wife, being great with child."

When Jennie had read through verse twenty, she closed the book softly, reverently, and there was silence in the room for a moment while everyone absorbed The Holy Words in their own fashion. The fire crackled in the fireplace, and outside a horse and buggy could be heard going down the street, its occupants singing "Joy To the World" at the tops of their lungs. Harry finally broke the silence. "Can we open our presents now, please?"

Mrs. Wade let out a chuckle, amazed that her impatient little son had waited as long as he had. The silence broken, everyone began talking at once, wiggling in their chairs, or getting up to stretch cramped muscles. Harry flew to the table that held their little Christmas tree. "Can I go first?"

John, with mischief in his eyes cried out. 'No! I'm going first this year. You go first every year!"

"No I don't! Samuel went first last year!"

"No, I didn't! I haven't gone first since this household was blessed with your presence," piped up Samuel, rising from the floor and stretching his back muscles. There was teasing in his voice as well, but Harry wasn't quick to notice.

"Boys, boys!" Mrs. Wade rose from the sofa and made her way across the room to the tree. She enjoyed a good joke as much as the next person but didn't want it to come to blows on such a day as this. "Harry, my dear, they are just teasing you. If you want to hand your presents out first, that's perfectly all right. Now go ahead."

One by one, the presents disappeared from beneath the tiny tree. John held up the flannel shirt made by his mother. Samuel seemed genuinely thrilled with his warm, wool socks, and Harry couldn't be happier with the wooden horse presented to him by his grandparents. Mrs. Wade had a new shawl, compliments of Jennie, and Georgia loved the two hankies prettily tatted by her mother. Grandma Filby was thrilled with her new slippers, hand-knitted by Georgia. Grandpa Filby was thanking John for the little bit of pipe tobacco, a real treasure these days. Georgia was agog over the new quilt for her bed, a joint effort from herself, their mother, and Grandma Filby. Jennie toyed with the new leather sewing thimble John had given her, all the while glancing from one smiling face to the next. Her heart felt over-flowing with blessings on this most Holy Day of Christ's birth. She was warm, content, and comfortable within the bosom of her family. Finally she realized that Georgia was starring intently at her. "What about you, Jennie, are you ready for one more gift now?"

The smile never left Jennie's face, though a slight frown wrinkled her brow. Her glance strayed back to the tree, thinking she might have missed some small package that had escaped her detection from her many other glances. But, no, there was nothing there. She watched as Georgia rose from her chair, crossed the room and inserted her hand inside the tree itself. Slowly, carefully, she extracted a neatly folded letter. In a voice, quiet, and trembling with emotion, she explained to her sister. "Jack sent this to me several weeks ago. He wanted me to save it for you as a surprise Christmas present. I assure you, I haven't read it." Georgia handed the neatly folded letter, tied in a bright red ribbon, to Jennie, who accepted it with shaky hand. "The ribbon was my touch," she added. "I think it helped to hide it well in the tree, don't you?"

"Yes, quite," whispered Jennie, fingering the letter like the treasure it was.

The solemnity of the moment, shared mostly between the two sisters, was broken by their teen-age brother, John, when he rose from his chair and headed for the kitchen. "Can I have some more of Grandma's Apple Pan Dowdy, Mama?"

"Me, too!" Harry was off like a shot, fighting to beat his older brother to the table. Suddenly Samuel was there, barring his way, and the playful fight ensued.

Mrs. Wade looked at her three sons, rolled her eyes, and asked the room in general. "Someone tell me again why I let those boys under the same roof at the same time, because I surely think I'm soft in the head." Laughter filled the room once more as the others slowly made their way towards the kitchen. Grandpa Filby helped his wife of sixty plus years to her feet. Georgia stopped by Jennie's chair, put her hand tenderly on her sister's shoulder, and looked knowingly into her face. "Everyone will understand if you want to sneak away and read your present, especially me. I'd give anything to have such a missive from Louis."

Jennie rose to her feet, tucking the treasured letter into the belt at her waist. "No. I think I'll wait until later when there are less distractions." Harry squealed as big brother, John, drove his knuckles playfully into his head. The two sisters looked at each other and smiled. "See what I mean?"

"I do indeed," agreed Georgia as she linked her arm through Jennie's and made their way to the kitchen.

The apple pie and/or apple pan dowdy, in some cases, was passed around. Laughter and conversation filled the room, reaching into corners where firelight and candlelight could not. Jennie joined in periodically, but tasted not a single morsel of whatever it was she ate. The letter, the precious letter from Jack, was burning like a live coal against her skin. She longed for this evening to end so she could rush to her room and read the words written by his hand and intended for her eyes only.

The scraping of chairs legs on the hard wood floor captured her attention as nothing else could at that moment.

"Harry, you look ready to fall asleep right there in your chair, dear. Why don't you go upstairs and get ready for bed." Harry willingly complied. His kisses good night to everyone in the room were automatic, and drained of emotion, the long day taking its toll on the usually vivacious seven year old. His actions brought a smile to the lips of everyone he came in contact with. But his waning energy was contagious, sending Georgia and his grandparents in search of frocks for their walk home.

Hugs and kisses were given all around, and thanks for the dinner and gifts. When the door finally closed, and the last good-bye still hung in the air, Jennie dashed upstairs to her room. Jack's letter was freed from its waistband confinement, the red ribbon hastily untied, and the letter carefully unfolded.

Winchester, Virginia
December 12, 1862

My dearest Jennie,

First of all, I beg you not to be mad at George for keeping this letter from you. I had not the means or way of getting a proper Christmas gift to you so thought the gift of myself in the form of this letter would just have to do. How I wish my words could be spoken and not written you cannot imagine. Or maybe you can. At any rate, it looks like the Rebels are going to keep us apart for still another holiday. I pray that next Christmas we can be together again, at last. But I do not like to think too badly of our enemy because thoughts of Wesley keep coming to mind, and I wonder where he is, what he is doing, and even if he is still alive. But I do not want to think too morbidly right now, but rather to think of you in happier times.

Though this letter is written weeks before the day of Our Savior's Birth, I can already think ahead and know what that day will be like for you. See if I don't get it right. You will be up early to help your mother with meal preparations. Then, like Christmas Eve, you and your family will walk the several blocks to St. John's Lutheran Church for services. There will probably be snow on the ground, but not too much. You'll have a wonderful meal with your family and open presents later in the evening. I'm thinking you might wait until everyone has gone to bed to read this letter. So, how am I doing so far?

As for me, it is hard to say what my Christmas Day will be

like. We are still marching all over this Shenandoah Valley and I have been under the weather as of late. It is nothing serious, but it has slowed me down some. I expect to be well enough in a few days, and certainly restored to full health by Christmas Day. That being said, my day will probably go something like this: there will be a church service, to be sure, and Cook will probably find something special to prepare for us. Some of us will still have to go out on patrol and guard duty, but the rest of us will have the day off to do whatever we please. Some will go off by themselves to write letters and think of home, and for them it will be a very sad day of reflection. Some will stay busy cleaning guns and equipment, and others will stay close to the fire and sing songs and tell stories. I plan to be in the latter group, at least that is what I am thinking right now. I miss you greatly, but I do not want to be melancholy all the day long, nor do I think you would want that for me. So if I stay around the fire with my brother, Ed, and some of the other boys from Gettysburg, we can probably manage to keep each other's spirits up. I hope! But there are certain songs we will have to avoid, otherwise it will get pretty quiet around that fire. We never sing "Home, Sweet Home," and I think "Silent Night" might bring on the doldrums just as quickly. Sometimes it seems that no matter what we do, there is always something to remind us of home, something that will make us wistful. Did you notice that I said 'we'? I said that because I find myself thinking of home more and more these days, especially with Christmas coming on. I think of what it was like before this terrible war started tearing lives apart and turning our world upside down. I long for it to be upside right again! And it will be for us again, one day, and I hope one day soon. One day soon I will be marching back to Gettysburg to stack arms for the last time, and then put my arms around you, forever this time. What do you have to say about a plan like that?

Well, my dear girl, I have to close this letter now or it will never get sent in time to surprise you, I hope, at Christmas time. Promise me that on Christmas evening you will sit and think fondly of me, because I will be thinking of you. In this small way we can pretend that we are spending the day together. So, until the day comes when we can spend our time together forever, I remain your..

Truest and best friend,
Jack

Jennie pulled Jack's letter close to her breast with one hand and reached for her hankie with the other. Tears flowed freely now, and for the life of her she couldn't decide whether they were tears of joy or sorrow. She missed Jack desperately, that's where the sorrow came in, but he had said that he wanted to spend the rest of his life in her arms. What sweet joy that brought to mind! Oh, was there ever a better Christmas present?

Jennie read through the letter from beginning to end one more time before carefully, reverently folding it and tucking it inside the daguerreotype case that held Jack's likeness. Tonight the picture stood on her bedside table, but in the morning it would find its way back inside her apron pocket where she could touch it throughout the day and be reminded of him who she held so dear.

Alone in her room, Jennie smiled through the last of her tears. A noise outside caught her attention, and curiosity made her move to the window to see what had caused it. A young woman had fallen in the snow and another was helping her to her feet. The young woman wasn't hurt, but neither was she thrilled to have the muddy, wet slush all over her garments. As the poor thing was brought upright moonlight glanced across her features and Jennie realized that it was Julia Culp who had fallen, and Annie Culp who had helped her back on her feet. She tapped on the windowpane to catch their attention and was thrilled when they heard her and looked up. Opening the window, Jennie called down. "Are you all right Julia?"

"Yes, I am. It's nothing a little soaking and brushing can't fix. Merry Christmas, by the way!"

"Oh, thank you! Merry Christmas to you, too! Have you got a moment?" Jennie didn't waste any time when the two sisters of her dear childhood friend, Wesley, nodded ascent and moved towards the front porch. Quickly, but quietly, so as not to wake anyone else in the house, Jennie made her way downstairs to the front door. Grabbing her wrap from its peg, she opened the door and stepped outside.

"Merry Christmas," she greeted again, and got the same in return. "Can I get you a rag to help wipe down your dress Julia?"

"Oh, no thank you," she answered. I have most of it wiped off now anyway, so it is of no consequence. Tell me, how did you spend your day?"

"We had a wonderful day spent quietly at home once we got back from morning services. Samuel brought us a leg of lamb for our dinner, which was first rate, and the boys had a good time teasing each other all the day long. That being said, I guess it wasn't that quiet of a day after all." Jennie giggled at her little joke and the Culp sisters joined in. "How about you two, what was your day like?"

Annie spoke up this time. "Ours was fairly quiet, too. Since losing Mama and Papa the celebrations just don't seem the same any more. We are on our way home from Mrs. Sheckley's house just now. The poor dear can't get out much any more and we took her a plate for her dinner tomorrow."

"What is the latest from Jack? Have you heard from him lately," inquired Julia.

Jennie's face lit up at the mention of his name, her smile easy to make out, even by the dim light of the moon. The two sisters smiled as well. "As a matter of fact, I received a letter from him this very day. He had sent it to Georgia to keep as a surprise for me and I couldn't have received a better Christmas present."

"Where is he now," Annie asked.

"I am not entirely sure, of course. They move around so much, you know, but this latest letter was addressed from Winchester, Virginia." Jennie paused for a moment, wondering if she dared ask about Wesley, or whether the very mention of his name would cause this chance encounter with her childhood friends to end on a sour note. The momentary pause lengthened into awkward proportions until finally Jennie gave voice to her concerns. "And what about our dear Wesley, have you heard anything from him by chance?"

Annie leaned in conspiratorially, while Julia glanced over her shoulder, afraid of being overheard. "We have heard nothing recently. But a few months back a letter reached us from someplace in Virginia. He is with their famous General Stonewall Jackson, so we watch for the general's name when it appears in the newspaper and have a little idea of where Wesley might be."

Jennie was thrilled to hear this bit of news. At least it proved Wesley might still be alive, though she understood why Annie and Julia couldn't simply shout it from the rooftops. Wesley was, after all, in the Rebel army. He was the enemy to all in the North, and the people of Gettysburg had more reason than the rest to hold him in contempt, since he used to be a native son. A chill rushed over Jennie, reaching from her spine to the small hairs on the back of her neck. The cold night air was getting to her, she suspected. Hurriedly she reached out to give her two friends a warm hug. "I'm glad I saw you passing by," she whispered.

"Me, too," said Annie. "Merry Christmas!"

"Merry Christmas," said Julia, as she released Jennie from their hug.

"Merry Christmas," called Jennie, as she closed the door softly on her retreating friends.

*   *   *

*   *

The fire felt wonderful against Wesley's skin. Fresh from guard duty, his musket was carefully stacked with the others in his company, and the young Confederate private was free to enjoy the warmth of a Christmas fire. His friend, George, handed him a cup of what was passing for coffee these days.

"Thank you kindly," said Wesley, accepting the cup with both hands, the better to warm them. Snow coated the ground here, near Fredericksburg, Virginia. Most of his comrades were sullen this evening, glad that the Christmas Day was finally coming to a close. Fresh from a terrible battle fought only a few weeks ago, there were vacancies around their various campfires, reminders of how fragile life was. Talk was sparse, most of the men lost in their own thoughts of home and hearth far away. Somewhere someone was singing softly, but Wesley couldn't make out the words, didn't recognize the tune.

The fire around which Wesley sat was burning low. He wished someone would toss on another log, he was too foot sore to search some out himself. He was wearing a new pair of socks inside a pair of brogans that were a tad too snug, all thanks to a dead Yankee from the battle a few weeks ago. Being the victor had its moments. He remembered the first time he had ever done that, gone through the haversack of a dead man, searching out food, ammunition, money, anything that could be of value. It had repulsed him at first, but necessity made it practical, even prudent. Before long, it was a commonplace act, something to look forward to. There were times when, if not for scrounging, he would have literally starved to death. No pay had come his way in over six months, and the way the quartermaster moved it was amazing they had an army at all. Still, good old Stonewall Jackson, that beloved, sometimes weird general managed to keep everything together. Wesley thought these boys around the fire would eagerly follow that man to Hell and back, and sometimes felt they had, if he would just say the word.

Something was crawling through Wesley's beard, and he instinctively reached up to scratch it, search it out and toss it into the fire. Lice, a constant companion ever since he joined up. It was the one thing to be counted on, even if you couldn't count on being paid or fed. His coffee cold now, he tossed the remains quickly down his throat, brought his blanket up closer around his neck and shoulders, and lied down to sleep. But sleep was a long time coming tonight. His friends around the fire were all sleeping, or so it seemed. Only Ben stayed awake, his hands turned to the fire and his eyes glazed over, deep in thought.

As much as he bid it leave him alone, thoughts of home teased Wesley tonight. And even in that teasing a war raged, for what home did he concentrate on, his boyhood home in Gettysburg, or the more recent one in Virginia? Gettysburg was so far in the past now he thought it might be unrecognizable, but there were certain things, when he thought hard enough, that were imprinted in his memory like the markings on a coin. He pictured Culp's Hill, as they called it, named after his uncle, and the perfect place for him, and his dear friends, Jack and Jennie, to play and picnic the summer days away. There were rocks to climb on and around, and logs to balance their way across. Jennie rarely made it all the way across, but only because Jack would tease her until she either fell or jumped down. Then, of course, he was right there to make sure she was all right. Wesley almost chuckled out loud at the very thought. As a youth he never could quite make out why Jack always behaved that way around Jennie, but later it all made perfect sense. Those two were destined for each other since childhood. It makes one wonder where they would be right now if not for this blasted war. The war! Everything always came back to the war! No stranger to battle now, Wesley still looked for Jack in the face of every Union soldier he met. Praise God they hadn't come across each other – yet. And, God help him, Wesley still didn't know what he would do if the moment ever came. He hadn't seen Jack in years now, not since he left Gettysburg to move to Shepherdstown, Virginia with Mr. Hoffman and his carriage shop. That was back in 1856, eons ago now, or so it seemed. It wasn't so bad at first because several of his Gettysburg friends had come with him, including Ed, Jack's older brother. But on that fateful day when war was declared, the Gettysburg boys had all headed back home, leaving Wesley alone in Virginia. The bile started to rise in his throat as he thought about it. *Why didn't I just go with them? Nothing good came from staying here!*

Wesley fought those memories back like a boy with a stick, refusing to let them get a toehold. But it seemed of no use, and instead of drifting back farther into his childhood, he moved into the not too distant past where all of his life-changing decisions were made. Decisions that changed his life forever, and not necessarily for the better. He'll never forget the looks on his Gettysburg friends faces when he told them he wasn't leaving, wasn't going to go back north with them. They didn't seem to understand that his job was here, his home here now. They argued, and in the end he walked out of the room, not wanting to defend his actions any more. It was a bitter good-bye, and now they'll probably never know how much he truly regretted it. They also didn't see him standing in the shadow of the blacksmith shop when they boarded the wagon that would take them all north, and out of his life forever. Just then, for a brief moment, he almost ran after them, calling out that he had changed his mind. But he didn't. Instead, he stuffed his fists into his pockets, turned, and walked away. It was such a different good-bye from when he left Gettysburg the first time. Then it was he doing the leaving, and his sisters staring after the departing wagon. The looks of regret were the same, however, and Wesley shivered in remembrance.

It was only a matter of months later when Wesley was interrupted from his work in the carriage shop by a loud commotion on the street. He looked out in time to see the general, the famous Stonewall Jackson himself marching into Shepherdstown, looking for recruits for the Confederate army. He wasn't the famous Stonewall just then though, that all came later. It was the knowledge of what Wesley knew now mingling with what was that made the image so much more poignant. He and his newfound Virginia friends didn't hesitate longer than it took to give notice to Mr. Hoffman before running to enlist. And now they were duly sworn members of Company B, Second Virginia Infantry Regiment. Like everyone else, they knew the war wouldn't last longer than the first battle, certainly not longer than a few months. *How foolish could any group of people be?*

Wesley rolled over, time to warm the other side by the fire. The fellows that were singing earlier had quieted now he noticed. Ben, who lay next to Wesley was softly snoring, and somewhere a coyote howled for a mate. He waited for the answer, and heard it way in the distance. Tired in body and soul, Wesley wondered why he was still awake. Usually comforting thoughts of home and family lulled him to sleep in mere minutes, but tonight it wasn't *home* that was calling him out, it was friends. And in those childhood friends he found regret. Regret for words unspoken, and decisions made that couldn't be taken back. Life changing regrets haunted him, howling through his mind like the coyote in the woods. Finally, restlessly turning back towards the fire, Wesley vowed to make it all right some day, somehow.

*   *   *   *

Jack ducked his head as he entered the roughly put together lean-to that had passed for home these last few weeks. The 87th Pennsylvania Volunteers were finally in winter quarters, however temporarily. Dropping a load of wood on the floor, he carefully placed several logs on the fire.

"Careful there, Jackie Boy, we have to make that load last us the rest of the night, and I, for one, don't want to sit through a bonfire now only to freeze to death come morning."

"Don't worry Billy. They just dropped off another load down at the end of the row, but don't ask me where they got it. I will tell you this though, it all looks suspiciously like fence posts, so I doubt that anyone expended themselves on cutting firewood tonight."

His chore completed, Jack wiped his hands on his pants and found a seat on the end of his bunk, at least that's what they jokingly called it. Their "bunks" were nothing more than their rolled up blankets, but ever since they joined the army they had learned it was best to put a good spin on things. Here, inside their tiny cabin, four Gettysburg friends found comfort against the winter weather, and solace in each other's company. They had known each other most of their lives, but hadn't really been close until the war brought them all together. Now, together in marching, drilling, eating, and sleeping, they had formed a unique bond, well aware of each other's faults, strengths, weaknesses, likes and dislikes.

"Hey, Jack." It was Billy again, "me and Will are thinking of getting a game of whist going. Are you in, or are you just going to sit there and think about that girl of yours?"

Jack didn't answer, but gave the two a look that passed for one.

Billy and Will chuckled, proud of their little joke. It had been a long, cold day, and everyone was homesick. Their meal of salted beef, beans, desecrated vegetables, and coffee had all who ate it dreaming of holiday meals back home. Cook had promised them something special for dinner on Christmas Day, but the wagons hadn't arrived in time so they were stuck with same old, same old. He did manage to find some fresh potatoes, however, and with added gravy, it really wasn't all that bad. At least no one walked away hungry. Some of the boys had received packages from home with cakes and pies baked by mothers or wives, and they eagerly shared what they had, though in most cases the goodies were a far cry from the way they would have been presented on the table at home. Cakes were crumbly, and pies dented in the middle, but it mattered little to the soldier nostalgic for home. They dived into the treats, sometimes without benefit of individual plates, while the true recipient apologized for the shape the item was in. And no one listened or even heard him, so thankful they were for eating the sweet.

Jack was indeed thinking about Jennie when Billy brought up the card game. He found himself doing it a lot more these days, and it filled him with a profound sense of something he couldn't quite put his finger on. He had learned many things since this war began, and one of those things was not to put too much stock in plans for the future. Too many times around the campfire he had heard the stories of men carrying furlough papers in their pockets, furloughs to go home, marry, and quickly return, only to be killed in battle the next day, the furloughs, like their dreams, never materializing. And so Jack bided his time. The thought that this war couldn't go on too much longer giving him the strength to stay the course, and let the future catch up to him. Although, with every day that passed, Jennie seemed to become more and more linked with that future, however out of reach it might seem for the moment.

Speaking of out of reach, Jack strained to reach his haversack where Jennie's daguerreotype lay safely hidden away. Pulling it out he stared intently at her for several minutes, studying features memorized long ago. The arrival of her picture hadn't come as a surprise, especially since she had told him of its coming, but it was still a most pleasant gift. Unlike her many letters, this daguerreotype was holding up much better. Of course, it helped that it wasn't folded so many times, the creases becoming more pronounced with each fold until it seemed the letter would simply fall apart in his hands. When it reached that point he preferred to retire it to a deeper corner of his haversack, resisting temptation and risking losing it all together.

Jack's older brother, Ed, came into the cabin, bringing a blast of cold air in with him. Billy and Will cried out as their cards went skidding across the makeshift table. Ed ignored them as he worked to close the rickety door.

Jack brought himself up to a sitting position. "Where you been Ed?"

"Me and some of the boys were sitting around a fire, talking."

"Talking about what?"

"Oh, you know, Ma's apple pie, roast goose, oyster stuffing, warm bread straight from the oven."

Ed would have gone on but Billy and Will were tossing cards in his direction, begging him to stop. "Ain't we been tortured enough this day? Do you have to go on, reminding us of what we can't have?"

"Sorry. It kind of helped us remember better times, times that will be back just as soon as we can bring this war to a close."

"Yeah? And just how long do you think that's gonna take? We already been at it for longer than the three months they promised us to begin with."

"Give it a rest, Will. We're all in the same boat. We all want to get back home as much as the next guy. We just gotta stick it out a might longer, that's all. Those Rebels are much worse off than we are, they can't possibly stand too much more. You mark my words, by this time next year we will all be sitting around our own hearths in Gettysburg getting fat on Mama's cooking. Now it's late, get those cards put away and get some sleep."

"Yes, sir, Poppa!"

Will ducked just in time to miss the tin cup that sailed in his direction. He chuckled at his little joke, and the way in which it was received. Billy joined in the laughter.

"Knock it off, you two! We're on first watch again in the morning and I, for one, want to get some shut-eye."

The cards dutifully put away, the four Gettysburg friends burrowed down into blankets to sleep. As full of mischief as Billy and Will seemed for a while, it was only a matter of minutes before soft snoring could be heard coming from their side of the tiny cabin. Jack fought the urge to crawl closer to the fire to write still one more letter to Jenny. His paper supply was running low, and he knew it would be too disturbing to Ed, Billy and Will if he started digging through his haversack at this late hour. No, Jenny can drift through his mind as easily as she can on paper. And so he drifted off to sleep, drafting a letter in his head. It began, *Dearest Jennie....*

Chapter 3

March 1863

"In everything give thanks: for this is the will of God
in Christ Jesus concerning you."
1 Thessalonians 5:18

Sunday church service was just getting over. The last hymn had been sung and people were closing their hymnals, replacing them in the box in front of them. Skirts rustled, and pews creaked, as the St. James Lutheran Church congregation members took their seats. From the front of the church Pastor Abraham Essick began his final announcements.

"My dear friends in Christ, if you are not already aware, our own President Lincoln has set aside tomorrow, the 30th of March as a National Day of Prayer and Fasting by official proclamation. It is a wonderful proclamation, and would that I had the time to read it to you in its entirety. But I won't, it being quite lengthy." There were a few sighs of relief, as well as stifled giggles as Pastor Essick looked over the tops of his spectacles at his flock. "If you would indulge me a few minutes I promise to keep it brief and to post it in its entirety on the back wall for all to read. Let me begin, 'And whereas it is the duty of nations as well as of men, to own their dependence upon the overruling power of God, to confess their sins and transgressions, in humble sorrow, yet with assured hope that genuine repentance will lead to mercy and pardon; and to recognize the sublime truth, announced in the Holy Scriptures and proven by all history, that those nations only are blessed whose God is the Lord. And, insomuch as we know that, by His divine law, nations like individuals are subjected to punishments and chastisements in this world, may we not justly fear that the awful calamity of civil war, which now desolates the land, may be but a punishment, inflicted upon us, for our presumptuous sins, to the needful end of our national reformation as a whole People? We have been the recipients of the choicest bounties of Heaven. We have been preserved these many years, in peace and prosperity. We have grown in numbers, wealth and power, as no other nation has ever grown. But we have forgotten God.' There is more, much more, my dear friends, and I invite you all to read it before going on your way today. I do not need to remind anyone sitting here today of the blessings God has bestowed upon us as a nation, as a town, as a people. So, please, join me tomorrow as we set aside this one special day as a full day of prayer and fasting. As you also know, these doors are always open to you, but tomorrow in particular, they will be open to anyone wishing to pray together as a united congregation."

Pastor Essick made the sign of the cross. "Now, go in peace."

The Wade family filed out of the church with the rest of the congregation. Pastor Essick, true to his work, had posted President Lincoln's full petition on the back wall, but so many people had gathered around to read it that it would seem to take forever for their own turn to come up. Instead, they stood in line to shake the pastor's hand, invite him to Sunday meal, which he declined today, and walk the few blocks home.

It was a beautiful spring day, full of the promise of budding flowers, even if the breeze still retained the sting of winter chill. Harry skipped on ahead of his mother and sister, leaving them to walk arm in arm, each of them lost in their own thoughts. The pastor's words had been powerful, full of the accusing finger of sin, but also of God's good mercy and Christ's redemption. These thoughts and words they knew, heard them every Sunday, and studied them each morning during private Bible reading. But it was the thought of the President of the United States asking everyone to join together in prayer for the common good of the nation that had them so moved today. If the simple prayer of one person can reach the ear of God, imagine what the combined prayer of thousands can accomplish. It was enough to give anyone pause.

A soft chuckle from her mother had Jennie looking in her direction. "What is so funny? Anything you care to share Mama?"

Mrs. Wade chuckled again. "I was just wondering if Harry knew what fasting meant, seeing as how we will be practicing it tomorrow and all."

Now it was Jennie's turn to giggle. "Too true. Knowing Harry, he probably thinks it has something to do with a foot race."

The two women looked at Harry running and skipping ahead of them down the street, full of youthful vitality.

Jennie whispered conspiratorially to her mother. "Do you think we should tell him? Or just wait until tomorrow morning when we serve him his tea for breakfast and he discovers that is all he's getting for breakfast."

Mrs. Wade laughed louder this time. "That would be fun indeed. But I don't think I want to contend with the temper tantrum after such an evil trick, do you?"

Jennie agreed. "Probably not. So I think I'll make an extra batch of biscuits today, that way we can all have something more on our stomachs before going to bed tonight."

My darling Jack,

I'm thinking of you today much more often than normal even. I don't know if you have heard about President Lincoln's request for this to be a day of prayer and fasting, but Pastor Essick told us about it in church yesterday and we are doing our best to make a good example. But it is hard. Mama and I decided not to force Harry and Isaac to fast with us, and that is what makes it so hard. This morning I fixed them eggs and ham to go with the biscuits I baked yesterday and the aroma almost made me cry out loud. Mama grabbed the laundry basket and went outside to hang the clothes on the line to escape the tempting smells. I told her that was very mean of her, and she told me to pray about it. But that is one thing no one has to tell me to do any more, pray I mean. I pray for you, I pray about the war, I pray about Georgia and her unborn baby, I pray about money to pay the bills, and oh, so much more. Mostly I pray about the war, because when that comes to an end everything else will fall into place. You will come home, the shortages will cease, and all will be right with the world once more. Don't you just wish it were so, my dear Jack? Oh, how I long for those days long past when we had no cares or worries. When we frolicked in the sun along the banks of Rock Creek, just the three of us, you, me and Wesley. But I know those days of our carefree youth will never come again, and I pray for those feelings of constant yearning most of all.

Looking back, I think I should probably tear up this letter and start from scratch. I believe the emptiness of my stomach is taking over my head and heart. Please don't think I am as melancholy as all that! Things are not all that bad in this household or in Gettysburg in general.

Tell me about yourself, Jack. Tell me what you have been doing lately. Are you still doing a lot of marching and drilling? Are you eating enough? Listen to me, there I go on about eating again! I'm terrible!

Do you remember me telling you about Isaac, the little boy we board during the week? Well he is an absolute angel. He and Harry get along better than even I had hoped. Of course Harry is in school most of the day, but when he comes home he immediately shares whatever he learned with his new friend, and the two of them are getting smarter every day. Talk about the answer to a prayer!

I am glad that spring is finally here. Somehow the trials that we are all going through seem lighter when the sun is shining and warm breezes drift through the house, cleansing it of stale, closed up, winter air. Mama and I are talking about what to plant in the garden this year. Both of us think that we should plant a bigger garden than last year in order to offset the food budget. It is funny to think that we don't have to feed Georgia now, but we do have to feed Isaac. We simply traded one mouth for another it seems! And that is all well and good.

Speaking of Georgia, Mama and I are both busy making clothes for the new baby in our spare time. Mama already has several pairs of booties set aside and is now working on a knitted cap. I have been saving scraps from some of our many sewing projects and am endeavoring to make a small quilt, one just the right size for a tiny baby. The boys are even discussing what they can do to make a gift for the baby when it comes, but they don't want any help from Mama or me, so I don't know what they are planning. Whatever it is, I'm sure Georgia will love it all the more for the effort those two will put into it. That baby, when it arrives, will not be wanting for anything, believe me.

Last week as I was reading through the Psalms, I was struck by how many times the phrase 'How long Lord?" kept repeating itself. I did not count them, but I know it was frequent. Each time I read those words I thought about the war beset upon us, and wondered the same thing the ancient Israelites did. How long Lord? How long before this awful war will be over? How long before our men will come home, leaving their swords behind and turning back to the plow? Only He, in His infinite wisdom, knows the answer to that and many more questions. That being said, I pray for a speedy end to this conflict on this of all days.

My candle is burning low, dear Jack, so I must close this letter for now. I pray that this is the last letter I ever have to write to you, that you will soon be on your way back home to me, where you belong, and where you will stay forever.

All my love,
Jennie

Winchester, Virginia
April 15, 1863

My dearest Jennie,

How I look forward to receiving letters from you! Your letters cheer me as nothing else can, and sad are the days when mail call comes around and there is nothing waiting for me from you. You may think this odd, since your letters are not worthy of news like an actual newspaper, but when I read your words I can hear your voice saying them aloud. I can see your smile when you say something silly, and your frown in anguish when you say something sad. These things keep me close to you, help me to feel your presence, and get through the days. I say days because I reread your letters until they threaten to fall apart at the fold, as I know I've told you before.

You ask me about drilling and marching, so obviously I have told you about that on many occasions too. Yes, we still do a lot of drilling and marching, but we do a lot of guard duty here too. Our numbers are few and there is a constant threat of the enemy in our midst or very close by, so we must be very vigilant at all times. We have been quite safe as most units are still in winter quarters, but with the spring weather comes new campaigns, so we must be very vigilant. I do not expect anything to come of it, and in any case, we are quite prepared should the enemy try anything against us.

I agree with your thoughts about 'How long, Lord, how long?' There is not a man here that would not willingly toss his musket aside and race towards home the instant this war comes to a close. But therein lies the problem, as the war is not yet over, and we must do our duty to God and our country. It would not do to quit this war right now as nothing has been settled between us and the Southern people. If we were to quit today, leaving things as they are, this war would only rise up again in due time, leaving those that have already shed their blood to have done so in vain, and causing the death of so many more to come. No, better to stay the course right now, see this awful evil through to its close and know that it will never rear its awful head again.

We are all delighting in the warmer weather coming on now. It is so nice to linger outside, rather than in the tiny stuffy cabins we built to get through the winter in. They are nice enough, and we truly welcomed them when the winter winds blew cold and strong, but now that spring is here and the temperature is climbing, we enjoy getting outside in the fresh air more often. Now it is not quite a chore to eat a meal around the campfire, write a letter beneath a tree outside, enjoy Sunday services in an outdoor meadow, or do the marching, drilling and guard duty I was telling you about. I know that all of those things we look forward to now will get old after a time and we will once more begin complaining about them. We people are a funny lot, and never content with anything for very long, wouldn't you say?

Some of the sickness that runs through camp in the winter is now abating, thanks in part to the warmer weather that draws us outside. So many men were sick with dysentery and the flux at one time it was hard to fill a respectable company. But now everyone is feeling much better, including myself. I had a nasty cold that would not release its hold on me for the longest time. I do not like to complain too much, but I am ever happy to have it gone now.

Mother sent a wonderful package awhile back filled with a pie, strawberry preserves, biscuits and other goodies. It did not last long, as you can well imagine. We shared it with some of the other men, so it did not last long. But some of the others also received packages from home, and they shared with us too. It makes the treats last longer that way, at least that is what we tell each other. We also receive packages from the Sanitary Commission occasionally, and they are always most welcome too. Anything, it seems, that breaks the monotony of camp life is embraced as a wonderful thing.

I have the image that you sent me of yourself and it, along with your many letters, are my greatest treasures. I keep them in my haversack because if we have to march on a moments notice my haversack is one of the first things I would grab and I would not waste a lot of time packing up my belongings. I have probably already told you this before too, but I cannot say it enough how much your letters mean to me. I treasure the letters, yes, but more than that I treasure the thoughts and memories of you that they invoke. You are a very dear person, Jennie, and not just to your mama, your brothers or your sister, but to me as well. Like you, I long for the day when this war will be but a memory, albeit it a bitter one, but a memory all the same. Then I will come back to Gettysburg with open arms, longing to wrap them around you and never let you go.

But it seems as if I have to let you go now. The bugler is

calling for roll call so I must close or be sited for insubordination, and we don't want that. Take care my darling girl. My thoughts and prayers are with you always, and until we can meet again I remain.....

Your ever faithful friend,
Jack

*   *   *   *

Jennie stomped out of Fahnestock's Dry Good Store, letting the door slam noisily behind her. Turning left onto Baltimore Street she quickly adjusted the bundle beneath her arm. It was lighter than she had hoped, the cost of goods being higher than she had anticipated. It was the war, she knew. The blasted war that had driven the price of everything straight through the roof! She never thought she would have seen the day when simple calico would cost fifty cents a yard. Fifty cents! Both of her brothers needed new shirts, so now she would have to forgo the work dress she had hoped to make for herself. She did not begrudge John and Harry their shirts, because they were both in desperate need, but a simple bolt of calico should never have cost as much as she had just had to put down.

Dust from the boardwalk puffed up with each angry step, tiny clouds of irritation following in her wake. A black squirrel scurried across her bath, but she paid it no mind. Normally attuned to everything in nature, a true gift from God, today she didn't notice the bright blue sky nor the finches singing their merry tunes, or even the robin upset with her for coming too near her nest. One step pounded into the next until she reached High Street, which she would have crossed without notice except for the horse and rider that came careening around the corner. The rider called out a "sorry, miss," but hurried on his way. It was then she became aware of someone calling her name.

"Jenny! Please, wait for me!" It was Julia Culp, hurrying to catch up, and tying her bonnet even as she ran. "Have you heard the news?"

Still preoccupied with the cost of goods at Fahnestock's Jennie was glad for an ear to bend. "No, I don't think I have. But I will tell you one thing, I don't know how much more of this war I can take!"

"But, Jennie, that's…"

"I have just come from the dry goods store and do you know what I had to pay for calico? Fifty cents a yard! Fifty cents! Can you believe it?" Jennie brandished the bundle like a weapon in front of her for emphasis.

"Jennie, please, this is important." Julia touched Jennie's arm, hoping the physical contact would finally gain her friend's attention. "I don't know if you've heard or not, but the Southerner's have just lost their beloved General Stonewall Jackson. He was shot by his own men at a place called Chancellorsville."

Jennie stared at Julia, frowning slightly, hearing the words, but recognition coming slower.

"Do you know what this means? It means the war can't be too far from over. Stonewall Jackson was one of their best generals, and without him they must surely have to think about quitting soon." Julia's grip on Jennie's arm tightened slightly. "That means that Wesley might be coming home, and Jack, too!"

Jennie's whole demeanor changed at the mention of

Jack's name. "Oh, Julia," she gushed. "That is the best news ever. But are you sure?" Aware of her surroundings for the first time since leaving Fahnestock's, Jennie glanced quickly around. Several wagons moved up and down Baltimore Street, raising clouds of dust as they passed. Two women chatted on the opposite corner, while another woman leaned from an upstairs window shaking a dust rag furiously. Two little girls dressed in calico played with a kitten in the adjacent yard, though the poor thing looked like it would give anything to be someplace else. Everything seemed so – normal! There were no newsboys hawking their papers, nor criers in the street announcing the latest war news, none of the usual hoopla that accompanied such momentous news. "Are you sure about this, Julia?"

"More sure than I've ever been about anything in my life. I just came from church after dropping off another basket of socks and mittens Annie and I made up, when I happened by the telegraph office. I heard the commotion inside and asked what was the matter. Maybe it was the panic in my voice, I don't know, but anyway, they told me about Stonewall Jackson's death."

"Wesley was in his unit, wasn't he?"

"Yes, he was." Suddenly grave, Julia let her arm fall from Jennie's. "We haven't heard anything from Wesley yet, I mean, how could we? But I'm sure he's just fine, I feel it in my bones. Any time now he'll be away from the war for good and coming back home to us."

Jennie reveled in her young friend's optimism, finding strength for herself at the same time. 'Home!' It was such a wonderful word, such a wonderful thought. Jennie gave Julia a quick embrace, and before they pulled apart the commotion at the telegraph office spilled out onto the street. Soon the whole town would know that about the great and fearsome General Stonewall Jackson. Suddenly aware of the incongruity of cheering over the death of a man, Jennie bade good-bye to her friend and hurried on her way. Thoughts of expensive calico gave way to those of the war's ending and Jack's homecoming. What would that truly be like? She realized that the ending of the war was easier to imagine than beginning a life with Jack, though both of them held all manner of hope, excitement, and anticipation. Though Jennie would never have wished for the death of any man, she realized that was the only way wars could ever reach a conclusion. Her fervent hope was that, with their beloved general gone, the Confederate army would quit the war very soon now, and life in Gettysburg and around the country could go back to the way it was before anyone ever heard of Fort Sumter, or Bull Run, Shilo, Antietam Fredericksburg, or any of the rest. Her pace picked up with each battle brought to mind. Names of friends who never made it back from those battlefields echoed through her head, and then she remembered that she had promised her mother to stop by the newspaper office and see if any new names had been added to the list of casualties from this latest one, Chancellorsville they were calling it.

Adjusting the package under her arm, and telling herself for the umpteenth time to stop dwelling on that which she could not change, Jennie stepped off the boardwalk and into the dirt and mire that was Baltimore Street. Navigating past the horse droppings she made it safely across the street and up onto the boardwalk on the other side. The list of those fallen in battle was several days old now, so the crowd that usually accompanied such a posting was nonexistent. Today only a few woman gathered to look, reread, and share each other's distress. Jennie knew the women by sight but not by name. They shared a common greeting and then stepped aside so that Jennie might glance over the list as they had just done. Any new names were always posted at the bottom of the original list, so Jennie dropped her eyes to that section. Her heart sank at the notice of George Harper, a young man from their church. The other names were not familiar to her, but she sent up a quick prayer for their families all the same.

The day was heating up by the time she hiked across

Baltimore Street once more and made the turn onto Breckinridge. She could see into the backyard as she approached the house, making note that it would be a good day for Harry and Isaac to get some weeding done in the garden.

Jennie entered the house through the tailor shop door, knowing her mother would be found there this time of day. She always loved that smell of new fabric, of freshly laundered clothes waiting to be picked up, and the sweet odor of oil on the sewing machine. And, as expected, her mother was indeed in the tailor shop, sitting in her sewing rocker with a pair of trousers across her lap. Her mother's fingers moved deftly in and out, in spite of the arthritic pain that constantly plagued her. Her mother barely glanced up as Jennie came through the door, her attention on John, standing in the doorway to the living quarters side of the house. They were having another argument about John's enlisting into the army.

"I swear, boy, I don't know where you get your information from, but I want it to stop right now. We have had this conversation thirteen times past the fourteen that was originally acceptable. Now let this be the end of it!"

"But I'm telling the truth, Mama. Ask Jennie, I'll bet she knows about it."

"You bet I know what, pray tell."

"I told Mama that the Confederates had done killed their own general, that Stonewall Jackson, they call him. Down in Virginia, at Chancellorsville they're calling it, he went over where he wasn't supposed to be and his own men took him for Yanks and fired on him. He's dead, I tell you, and that mean's the war might soon be over, and here I am standing here, missing the whole thing."

Jennie's mother snorted in response, but never took her eyes off her sewing.

"It's true, Mama, I heard it from Julia Culp who had just come from the telegraph office."

Mrs. Wade was finally persuaded to put down her

sewing and glance up at the young people in the room. Her expression was not a happy one. "And don't you think that you're putting just a bit too much glory and power on one man's shoulders, young man? It's fuss and nonsense, I tell you, believing that the death of one man can mean the end of the war coming on. Fuss and nonsense!"

Jennie realized that this battle was between mother and son, and wisely kept silent.

"I'm seventeen now Mama, a full grown man, and I ought to be able to do what I want. And I want to defend my country like all of the other men in this town, not stay at home hiding behind women's skirts."

"You're not hiding from anything, son. I need you here, under this roof, helping out around here. Would you leave this household full of defenseless women and children?"

"You are certainly not defenseless Mama, and nothing ever happens in this town anyway."

"That is not true, young man! Did we not have this same conversation last year when the whole of the Southern army marched as close as Cashtown, scaring everyone out of their wits, and burning and pillaging as they went?"

John's shoulders slumped dejectedly ever so slightly, and just as quickly rose up defiantly. "I'm going to enlist in the army Mama, just as soon as I can find the recruiter for new troops. I'm sorry to go against your wishes and that's the truth of it, but I feel honor bound to do this thing."

Jennie watched the emotions play across her mother's face. The muscles in her jaw flexed several times, and her nose dilated as if she couldn't get enough air. Her eyes never left her son's face. There was silence in the room for several minutes, while the two combatants faced each other across the space of the nine-foot room.

John was the first to speak. "Please Mama, I really don't want to go against you. I need your blessing on this."

Finally, reluctantly, Mrs. Wade held her arms out for her

son's embrace. John hurried to return it, thrilled that he had, at long last, gotten the permission he had been searching for. But he was the only one smiling in the room. Mrs. Wade was the first to pull away, reaching for a hankie in her pocket at the same time. "You'd best be getting along then," she said, her words barely above a whisper.

John replaced the cap upon his head and moved towards the door, in a hurry now. As his hand reached the knob he paused momentarily, and without turning around, said, "thank you, Mama." The soft closing of the door muffled the sound of his mother's sobs.

Chapter 4

Monday, June 15, 1863

The Battle of Carter's Woods

"These things I have spoken to you, that in Me you may have peace.
In the world you will have tribulation;
But be of good cheer,
I have overcome the world."
John 16:33

Jack lay in a trench, sleeping the sleep of the exhausted. The Rebels attacked two days ago. At first everyone thought it was a small force of infantry with a few light artillery pieces, but they quickly discovered that a main body of the Confederate army was just beyond their protected confines of Winchester. Whispered words of "seeing the elephant" were soon passed up and down the line, as if it were some sort of childish story or game, and not the horrid reality it was turning out to be. And if that wasn't enough, it stormed hard all night long the night the Confederates first attacked. Jack's unit, the 87th Pennsylvania Volunteers, was marched to and fro wherever needed these past several days. Food and rest becoming secondary as the need for survival became the order of the day. Darkness came hard, quick, and total on Sunday night, and with the silencing of the heavy guns, many were the eyes that closed in unbidden relief, their muskets still clenched in their hands.

As Jack closed his eyes on the horrors of the day, the acrid smell of gun smoke, unwashed bodies, wet wool, and damp earth assailed his nostrils, and the moans of the wounded, the clanking of metal, the neighing of horses filled his ears. Someone mentioned the word elephant one more time, and that was the last that Jack heard. Sleep came quickly, as did the vision of an elephant. *Monstrously huge, it appeared out of dense smoke, marching straight for him. In the dream it never occurred to him to run, or even turn away, he simply stood there, stupefied, as it marched closer and closer. Then, at the last instant, just when he thought he would certainly be crushed by its gigantic feet, it sailed over the top of his head and was gone. The mammoth-sized elephant glared fiercely at him with bright red eyes, so bright that he felt the need to shield his own from the glare. Yet, when his hand came up to protect his eyes from that penetrating stare he suddenly realized that the elephant wasn't alone. There were two riders on the beast! Jennie rode unsteadily on its back, her long skirt flapping out and over the back of the elephant, she seemed not to see Jack at all. And, just as the beast disappeared over Jack's head, he became aware of the second rider, Wesley, hanging onto the tail as if his life depended on it. He, too, acted as if he didn't know Jack was even there.*

Someone called Jack's name. It was Ed, his brother, and there was an urgency to his tone that had Jack rubbing his eyes to clear his head. It was still pitch dark, but men were moving about everywhere, gathering gear, grabbing muskets, stretching the sleep out of their limbs. No one spoke beyond a whisper, and Jack finally leaned towards Ed, who was standing alert, watching over the rest of the company. "What's going on?"

"We're moving out. Don't take anything you can't carry quietly. And no talking once we get moving. And hurry up about it!"

"Where're we headed?"

"Harper's Ferry, I think, but we gotta get moving right quick about it, before the Rebels find out what we're about. Now come on, and no more talking."

Jack rolled up his blanket, tying it quickly, expertly, like he'd done so many times in the past. In an instant it was tossed over his shoulder, his haversack was readjusted, his musket snatched up and he was in line with the rest of them. It was a dark night, with not much of a moon to light their way. Crickets, insects and tree frogs helped to cover whatever noise the men might have made while preparing to march. Jack yawned once more, wondering how it was possible to be this alert after so little sleep. Their time in Winchester had been delightful, idyllic even, except for these past few days when the Rebels came knocking on the door determined to take back the city still one more time. He couldn't help but feel for those towns people. What was it one of them said, that the city had changed hands more times than he had fingers and toes for counting? And now here they are, leaving them to the ravages of the Southern army still one more time.

Jack was marching beside Willy, each of them doing their best to put one foot down in front of the other as quietly as possible. The Rebels were out there, somewhere, probably sleeping, best not to wake them up just yet.

"How far is it to Harper's Ferry, Jack?"

"Too far. Now be quiet."

"I'm really getting tired of all this, ain't you?"

"Yes. Now be quiet!"

"What time do you reckon it is?"

Jack never got the chance to answer. They had been on the march for over an hour when the first weak rays of light tried brightening the eastern sky. Robins, finches, cardinals and other songbirds began welcoming the new day, singing a hallelujah chorus to God, their maker. It had been a balmy night, almost too warm for marching, but with the coming day the men were finally coming into their own. The ranks were quiet, it being easier now to see where they were putting one foot in front of the other. Suddenly, from somewhere up ahead came the distinctive sound of musket fire. The men kept up their marching pace, but were infinitely more alert now. As quickly as it began, the firing subsided, but only momentarily. There were whisperings in the ranks, and most heads were facing in the direction of the recent commotion, though there were those few who couldn't take their eyes from the woods to their right. With the coming dawn "figures" could be seen in amidst the brush and small trees of the forest, made more intense with the recent firing and the knowledge that the Rebels had not left the area as yet.

Then, just when they thought the boys up ahead had gotten things under control the firing began again, more intense this time.

The order came down to get off the road and into the ditch along side. No one questioned the wisdom of this order as Minnie balls whisked overhead, slamming into the dirt of the road at their feet. Some of the bullets found softer targets in the limbs and bodies of those in Jack's company, adding their screams to the chaos. Jack made it into the ditch unscathed, but for the mouth full of dirt he consumed upon impact. Spitting and chocking to clear his mouth, he quickly raised his musket to take aim at the oncoming Rebel soldiers. At this point most of Jack's moves were not thought through, merely automatic. Fire the musket! Cock the hammer, open the pan, rip the paper cartridge with his teeth, prime the musket, close the frizzen, add the powder, ball and wadding, remove the ramrod. Fire the musket! Repeat, repeat, and repeat.

The early morning singing of the birds was lost in the cacophony of screams, and shouts, musket firings, and the squealing and neighing of horses. Soon the smoke from so many muskets filled the air like a blanket preventing anyone from seeing anything beyond the barrel of their own gun. It stung their eyes, and that familiar stench of gunpowder clung to their nostrils. Horses could be heard dashing down the road and across the field in their front, some of them riderless. And still Jack kept up the automatic motion of firing, loading, repeating. Commotion seemed the order of the day, and he wished with all his heart that he could get a drink of water.

Something fell heavily across his legs, pinning him to the ground. Jack fired his musket into the air, his aim disrupted from the added jostling of his body. Turning around to wiggle free, he realized that his friend, Billy, had been hit. As Billy howled in pain, Jack did his best to free his trapped legs. The blood on Billy's coat showed the wound to be near his shoulder, and after a quick examination, the wound proved to be more of a graze than anything serious. It was the shock of the pain that had Billy falling backwards. Jack leaned down over Billy's prone body. Their faces were coated in dirt and smoke, and perspiration made tiny, clean traces as it ran down into their necks. Around them the battle still raged. The musket firing was nonstop, as were the shouts and screams from their fellow soldiers. Across the way they could hear the howls coming from the enemy soldiers. Jack had never heard the ear piercing scream of an Indian war hoop before, but that is how he imagined it might sound.

Billy reclaimed his composure in a matter of seconds, once he realized his wound was nothing serious. Pushing Jack out of his way, he hurried to get back into the action. A second later a ball went through Jack's kepi, knocking it off his head. Instantly he ducked back into the ditch, said a quick prayer, and reached frantically for his musket.

The sun rose higher in the sky, but no one on the battlefield took notice of it, mostly because they couldn't, obliterated as it was from the smoke of so many muskets and cannon fire. Jack reloaded his musket for the umpteenth time, the motions coming so automatic now he didn't even think about it, just reacted. Fire! Load, and fire again! Most of the time he didn't even know what he was firing at, there was certainly no aiming going on. Who could see through all of the smoke? The soot and dirt coated everything, from clothing to faces and hands. He could feel it on his teeth, knew it was in his nostrils, and felt certain it had to be in his ears. Everything was in his ears! The constant firing of so many muskets, including his own, and in such close proximity was like a physical wave washing over him and never receding. Soon it became a constant ringing, or was it a high-pitched whine, he couldn't really tell. And wasn't sure he wanted to pay it any more heed. He was running low on everything now, from powder to caps, and still Jack stayed in that ditch firing into the nothingness that was smoke and Rebel screams for what seemed like days until someone jostled him, pulling at his shoulder. He turned to see their Captain Phillips screaming at him and the others around him, but no words were coming from his mouth, at least none that Jack could hear. The man seemed frantic, waving his arms and trying to lead them back, away from the ditch. It took only a few moments for Jack to realize that the man wanted them to fall back, back across the road and into the woods on the other side. For the briefest of moments Jack debated the wisdom of leaving the fragile security of this ditch, this safe haven that had become like a second home. But the others had picked up on the order, and he had to go. Why did he get the feeling they were going from the frying pan into the fire?

It was a retreat, and not a very smooth one. The Rebels had come up to within fifty yards of the protective ditch, one could almost see the fresh smoke from their muskets, even if you couldn't make out the soldier doing the firing. The screaming was so intense now Jack could almost taste it. It was then that he realized the scream was coming from his own throat, wasted energy he thought, and didn't care. He kept up the screaming until they were safely across the road and into the relative safety of the woods.

The captain had disappeared, but whether he was wounded, dead, or off somewhere leading others to safety Jack couldn't be sure. There were little pockets of fighting men everywhere in the woods. And there were bodies. There were bodies left behind them in the ditch, upon the road, behind trees and logs, and bodies that impeded their progress. Twice Jack stumbled over some poor soldier's legs or torso in his blind rush to catch up to the others.

Finally Captain Phillips was there again, pointing to a massive fallen log near several very large boulders. It didn't need much coaxing to get the men up and over the log and into the safety of the rocks. Captain Phillips was still behind them, shouting out his orders. But no one had to tell them to do what they had been doing all morning, if it was still morning. Cock the hammer, open the pan, tear the paper off the cartridge, prime, close, powder, buck and ball, wadding, replace ramrod, and fire! Fire! Fire!

Confusion seemed the order of the day, no matter how many other orders Captain Phillips or any other officer might shout. Ever since the first Rebel volley reached their ears chaos became their leader. It led them first on one side of the road, then the other. It led them from the road and into the woods. And now it was leading men to do whatever their hearts told them to do. But it probably wasn't even their hearts they were listening to, so much as fear. Before Jack could quite comprehend what was going on, men were once more bolting for the rear. Some simply tossed their muskets aside, running pell mell, like wild horses on a stampede to wherever their legs would take them. They jumped swiftly and gracefully over fallen logs, bodies, and anything that got in their path, to the point of shoving those that didn't run fast enough. The fact they were retreating was clear enough, but this was more than a planned, thought out retreat. This was a panicked rout!

The soldier to Jack's right, he didn't even know his name, didn't recognize his face at all, suddenly stopped firing. "Nuts to this," he said to no one in particular, and grasping his musket in both hands, jumped up and ran farther into the woods behind them. Soon several others who had found shelter behind the fallen log and rocks with Jack were taking up the same notion. In a matter of minutes Jack realized that if he didn't get moving himself, he would surely be left behind and killed. Or worse still, captured!

Clutching his musket, Jack looked over the log one more time. Smoke was enveloping the woods just like it did the road. Were it not for the zing, zing of Minnie balls flying through the air, and the plunk, plunk as they hit trees, shrubs or bodies, it could almost be called a pretty scene. The sulfur smoke clung mostly to the ground, drifting up gently, wafting really, into the lower branches of trees like fog in the first days of spring. It would be easy to simply stay here, cower behind the log and – zing! Plunk! A Minnie ball tore into the log directly in front of Jack's face. Little splinters of wood ripped into his cheek, just missing his eye. No hesitation now, Jack jumped up, running for all he was worth. He had no destination in mind, simply getting away from the madness. There was no order any more anyway, no one to lead or follow. It was like playing tag when they were kids, all you had to do was outrun whoever was "it" before they could tag you.

And then he felt it. He had been tagged! A sharp pain, like nothing he had ever experienced before, seared through his upper right arm, shattering the bone and sending fragments of his own body into the air and onto his face. He stumbled, falling to the ground in a headlong heap, the arm useless by his side. Stunned, Jack lay there for several seconds, recovering his breath and trying to make sense of it all. The pain was intense. It seemed to him that his arm throbbed with each beat of his heart, keeping perfect rhythm. His ear was pressed to the ground, just the way he had fallen, and he found it interesting that he could feel rather than hear the others as they rushed by, trying to find their own way to safety or the next line of defense. Slowly it dawned on him that they were leaving him behind, and this he couldn't bare. Jack made a feeble attempt to rise, when suddenly a boot pressed into his back, forcing him back onto the ground. "Stay where you lie, Yank!"

*   *   *   *
    *   *

Wesley Culp heard the beginning sounds of battle about the same time Jack did. He hadn't slept a wink all night because word had filtered down that the Yanks might try to escape and it was their job to stop them. And so they marched. They marched up the hills, down the hills, into the town, away from the town, down the road and into the woods. They were the Stonewall Brigade, it's what they did – march! He knew there were other regiments that thought his brigade actually enjoyed marching all over God's creation in all kinds of weather, with or without shoes, and many were the times Wesley wished for just five minutes alone with each and every one of them. He'd show them what he thought of marching. March all over their face, that's what he'd do! Just because they were darn good at what they did, didn't mean they particularly liked it, least wise not all the time.

The past week they had done more than their fare share of marching and fighting, living up to their sobriquet of Stonewall Jackson's Foot Cavalry. Word had filtered down that they were about to head north, into the land of good and plenty. Plenty! Plenty would be good. Wesley's stomach growled at the very thought of food, good food, enough to fill his belly all the way up for once. Wesley had no idea where up north they might actually be heading, but he couldn't help hoping that they might get close enough to Gettysburg for him to sneak away and say hey to his family, or what was left of them, that is. His father had died the same year Wesley left Gettysburg for life in Virginia, and his mother died towards the beginning of the war. Wesley always regretted that he hadn't been around to see her in her last days, nor to comfort his sisters when she passed. But such was life as a soldier in the Stonewall Brigade. It occurred to him, too, that Jack was more than likely wearing the blue uniform of a Union soldier now, so it would definitely not be a good thing to run into him. But what about Jennie, he wondered. Wouldn't it be fun to see her again after all these years? A smile flashed briefly across his face at the very prospect of seeing family and friends one more time.

He had been thinking on the intricacies of marching into his old hometown wearing the uniform of a Rebel soldier, and the wisdom of such an action, when the first sounds of battle reached his ears. It sounded quite a ways off, maybe over a mile or so. Several mounted officers went racing by, screaming at them to pick up the pace. "Come on, you foot cavalry! Let's go! You're needed up ahead! On the double quick, march!"

All thoughts of sleeping, eating and sneaking into his hometown were forgotten as he hurried to put one foot in front of the other and keep up with the others in the rank. He was winded by the time they arrived on the scene, but not nearly as worn out as in past marches. The fighting, as he approached, was intense. Those Yanks weren't going down quietly!

Wesley heard the cheers from some of the other Rebel units as his Stonewall Brigade joined their ranks, but he didn't take it personally. They had arrived to such cheers before. It was the same welcome all reinforcements received when they arrived during the heat of battle. A few hats were tipped in recognition, but soon the cheers blended with the famous Rebel yell, and they stormed into the fray like hounds after their prey.

The Yanks were being chased across a road and into the woods directly behind them. It was embarrassing really, the way they simply broke ranks and ran helter skelter in every direction regardless of where their individual units might be. Dense smoke denied him a good view of what was transpiring, but he watched as battle flags from both sides rose high above the smoke one minute and filtered back down like a pebble disappearing into a stream the next. Wesley saw movement in the cloud of smoke ahead of him. Lifting his musket to his shoulder, he quickly took aim and fired. He found it was actually easier this way, firing into the obscurity of smoke. It left you with the impression that you were doing your duty to country, but maybe God was sparing the ultimate receiver of your bullet. Kneeling down in the dirt, Wesley went through the same motions that Jack did to reload his musket, take aim, and fire again. After several minutes the motion became automatic, like marching late into the night when no thinking was necessary. *Just put one foot in front of the other Wes!*

At some point Wesley realized there were less and less bullets whizzing past his head, and his own unit had picked up speed as they moved aggressively forward. Somewhere an unseen officer was yelling at the top of his lungs. "That's it boys! We got 'em on the run! Up! Up! After 'em now!"

The famous Rebel yell filled the air, intoxicating the soldiers as they raced forward to the road, across it, and into the woods on the other side. It took only minutes to accomplish the move and they were almost saddened when they were greeted by the white flag of surrender just as they entered the trees. Wesley kept his musket at ready while several others cautiously approached the small band of Yanks that had gathered around the makeshift flag of surrender. But there were still others who were trying to run away, and Wesley quickly took up pursuit.

Briars and branches tore at his clothes as he ran through the pines, jumping over downed trees and protruding rocks. And bodies! Does anyone ever get used to seeing dead bodies littering the ground, he wondered. He hurled over one now, his sights on a living Yank trying his best to outdistance his pursuer.

Then another one came into view, and another. One of them went down, shot in the arm by another soldier off to Wesley's right. Wesley ignored him as he kept up his own pursuit, but he heard his comrade's triumphant cry as he dodged past. "Stay where you lie, Yank!"

*   *   *   *
*   *

The battle was over, but not the work. Wesley was thrilled to see that his friends Ben and George had made it safely through the fray, none the worse for wear. George, kneeling near the biggest oak tree he had seen in a long while, was busy going through the haversack of a poor, unfortunate Yank who was nowhere to be found. Several others were doing the same, and Wesley was just about to join in the treasure gathering when he heard Ben calling his name.

"Wes! Over here! Help us herd these here Yanks back to the road, will ya?"

Taking the time to whip a hankie from his pocket to wipe his face, Wesley slowly moved towards Ben and the twenty or so prisoners that had been rounded up. Ben and two other's from their unit had the prisoners in a sort of circle formation and were trying to get them to move in the direction of the road they had recently fought over. All of the prisoners had their hands in air, having been divested of muskets, haversacks, and anything else of value. The pile of goods continued to shrink as the victorious Rebel soldiers helped themselves to muskets, ammo, and haversacks filled with tinned meat, crackers, bacon, writing supplies, extra socks, shirts, and more personal items than they had seen in a long time. Wesley glanced in their direction as he wandered towards Ben, noting the smiles on some of their faces. More than one of them brought up the word Christmas.

"Quite the bunch, ain't they," Ben commented, pointing towards the prisoners with his musket.

At that Wesley tore his eyes away from the pile of overstuffed, welcoming haversacks to the business at hand.

"Look at 'em. They sure are a sorry looking lot, if you ask me. Some of 'em look ready to run again and the rest look ready to fill their pants. I wonder which its gonna be?"

Wesley looked at their faces now and realized it was true. Some of them glared back, nostrils flaring, and you could just see the fight that was still in them. Others were nervous, their eyes darting quickly from one direction to the next, looking for, what, help, he wondered. Then there were those that looked close to tears, the defeat clearly visible, and obviously the knowledge of what awaited them in whatever prisoner of war camp they were destined. About the only thing they had in common was the dirt that covered them from head to toe. Loathe to move at all, Ben had to scream at them and brandish his musket before he could get them to start for the road.

The gathering of prisoners was only one of many little dramas unfolding in the woods. While Wesley and Ben acted as guards, others nearby were tending to the wounded on both sides. Those that could walk were rounded up and marched off as prisoners of war, the others were left where they lay, waiting for stretcher bearers to take them to the nearest hospital.

Wesley was glad to notice the heavy smoke that had enveloped all of them since the rising of the sun had finally dissipated. The big guns had stopped belching their deadly missiles, and the muskets had, for the most part, stopped adding to the noise and bedlam of the day. But he had seen it all before, heard it all before, and smelled it all before. As sure as he was standing in the cool of these woods right now, Wesley knew it would all be repeated again, on another day, somewhere down the road.

The prisoners were finally on the move, resigned temporarily to their fate. But that didn't mean that the victors should let down their guard. He, Ben and the others kept their muskets trained on the circle of Union soldiers, hoping they wouldn't do anything so foolish as try to escape. Ben suddenly aimed his musket in the direction of two prisoners who looked to be talking to each other, their heads leaning conspiratorially close.

"You there! Keep you traps shut, if you know what's good for you!"

The two offenders looked over their shoulders in Ben's direction. One of them glared, the other looked completely unconcerned. Wesley realized that they were two of the nostril flaring Yanks he had noticed upon first approach. It was obvious to anyone who cared to look that there was still a lot of fight left in those two. But to their credit they did as they were told, however temporarily, and closed their mouths. Wesley couldn't help looking in their direction, admiring their strength and determination. He hoped they held onto that, because they would need it where they were going.

As Wesley continued herding the Union prisoners towards the road, now visible through the thinning pines, he thought he heard someone else calling his name. It was soft as first, hesitant even, as if whoever was doing the calling wasn't sure it was him. Wesley continued walking behind the prisoners, his musket still aimed in their direction, but now his head began turning left and right, looking for the owner of the voice. He turned just in time to see another group of Yankie prisoners being collected against the backdrop of a large bolder. Two of them looked wounded, lying as they were on the ground, but the one with the voice was staring intently in Wesley's direction, as still uncertain of his identity. He called Wesley's name one more time, a real question this time, and was just about to suffer the consequence of being hit with a musket butt when Wesley suddenly recognized the owner of the voice.

"Stop!" He screamed at the soldier who was still in the process of raising his musket to full shoulder height, the better to ram the Yankee. But it was too late. Battle adrenaline was still coursing through that soldiers veins, causing him to seek out any reason for continuing his murderous attack against any Yankee still standing. The musket butt came down hard on the Yankee soldier, but he had seen it coming and ducked at the last moment, saving himself from the full brunt of the swing. Instead of landing on his skull, which is what the Rebel soldier had in mind, it glanced off his ear and onto the back of his shoulder. But it was still enough to send him reeling. The voice went down like a rock, his arm up to deflect any more blows, but Wesley was there to put a stop to any more swings of adrenaline rush.

"Whoa! Whoa! Whoa!" Wesley grabbed the barrel of the musket - a big mistake as it was still hot from firing - and forced the gun to the ground. He didn't recognize his fellow soldier in arms as he was from another unit. The fellow looked mad enough to turn his musket on Wesley himself at first. But Wesley had brought his own musket up to shoulder height and was using as leverage against the man's chest. Eye to eye, Wesley watched as recognition slowly dawned across the man's face, the realization that Wesley was a fellow Confederate soldier and not intent on freeing one of the captives. Something akin to embarrassment flashed briefly across the man's face. He gave a quick but determined shove against Wesley, putting distance between them, before turning his attention once more to the voice on the ground.

"I said no talking! Didn't I say no talking, Yank? You try something like that again and I'll put this here musket butt straight through your dang blamed skull, and don't think for one minute that I won't!"

Wesley knelt down in the dirt beside the voice. The man was holding his ear, his face losing the contortion of pain it carried when he first went down. Wesley pulled a hankie from his pocket and used it to wipe the grime from the voice's face. He still didn't recognize the fellow, but there was something there, something he couldn't quite put a finger on that drew him to this man. At first glance he seemed taller than Wesley, which wasn't hard as Wesley was a few inches below normal height, and the voice had more meat on his bones, which also wasn't hard considering he was wearing the uniform of a Yankee soldier. Beyond that he was as dirty and unkempt as anyone else on this battlefield. It took a trained eye to recognize one's friends or fellow soldiers under these circumstances. The way a man stood, or walked, or wore his uniform was all anyone had to identify friend or stranger.

Wesley wiped the last of the grime from the voice's face, recognition slowly dawning as he looked into the eyes of his childhood friend. "Ed? Ed Holzworth! Is that really you?"

"It is for certain, last time I checked anyhow." Ed gave Wesley a weak smile and tried to pull himself into a sitting position. "It's been a long time."

"Too long." Wesley agreed. They stared silently at each other for several moments, lost in the wonder of seeing each other again after so many years. "My gosh, but you're a sight for sore eyes!"

"Well, you have the 'you're a sight' part right. I can't remember when I last had a proper bath or a shave." Ed reached up and wiped his hand across a three-day stubble on his chin. Out of the corner of his eye he glanced up at Wesley. "Peers to me, it's been awhile since you indulged yourself."

Wesley noted the twinkle in his friend's eye, remembering the bantering from childhood. Under other circumstances he would have wrestled him back to the ground, sharing punches as well as words. But these weren't ordinary circumstances, and his fellow soldier quickly reminded him of that when he reached down to grab Ed by the shoulder. "On your feet Yank! We got us some marching to do!"

"Wait! Wesley, do me a favor, will ya? Jack Skelly is here, wounded, over by that tree. Can you help him?"

Wesley watched as his friend was marched away with another group of prisoners, eyes widened in shock. Two friends, here, in one day, it was amazing! Turning quickly, he looked in the direction where Ed pointed. There were at least a dozen men, all but one wearing the blue uniform of a Union soldier. "Jack," he screamed. "Jack!"

One of the soldiers turned his head and looked in Wesley's direction. He was propped up against a young oak tree, the trunk of which was shared by two other wounded soldiers. Jack was holding his left hand over a gashing hole in his right shoulder. Someone had given him a rag or hankie to apply to the wound, but it was already soaked through. His face was pale from the loss of so much blood.

Wesley ran the short distance to the tree, and for the second time in mere minutes he dropped to the ground on his knees beside a wounded friend. His words came out in a whisper. "Jack, what have we done?"

Wesley used his limited amount of resources to get Jack to a surgeon as quickly as possible. Jack was carried by stretcher back to town, where a make shift hospital was set up in the Taylor House Hotel. It wasn't until later in the evening when he was finally able to speak to his friend.

He found Jack in a room with six other recovering Union soldiers, several of which looked as if they were staring death in the face. Jack looked only slightly better than he did when first encountered in the woods. His face was still pale from loss of blood, and now there was a huge bandage over his shoulder and right arm. He was sitting up on his cot, propped against the wall and looking listlessly at some far point on the opposite wall. His prospects now as a wounded prisoner of war were grim indeed, and Wesley couldn't imagine what was going through his head.

There was a chair in the corner, and Wesley quickly commandeered it, hauling it over close to Jack's cot. Jack saw him coming, turned, and forced a smile. Out of deference to the other wounded, they kept their voices low.

"Hey, Jack, it's been a long while."

"Too long."

"Never thought our first encounter would be like this though. Hate to see you like this."

"Hate to be like this, to tell you the truth." Jack's face lost the smile he had worn when Wesley first walked in, but Wesley didn't take it personally. It was obvious that Jack was still in a lot of pain. Wesley, in some small way, wanted to take his mind off of that.

"When was the last time you were home Jack?"

"Not since I enlisted. So it's been a few years now."

"Hear much from the folks back home? I mean, how are things?"

"Well, mostly I get letters from my mother, but my brothers write once in a while too. They're okay. They complain about the cost of everything going up because of this here war, but they'll make do." A bitterness crept into Jack's tone just then, taking some of the fun out of seeing a close, childhood friend again after so many years apart. Wesley didn't know what to say next. Not for the first time did Wesley think that no good was going to come from this war, no matter how it ended.

Jack sat on the cot, staring at that massive, spider-like crack on the opposite wall. Funny how the thing almost looked like a map of Gettysburg, with its roads spreading out in every direction, beckoning, calling him home from wherever he might be. But he couldn't think of that right now. Wesley, his friend, the enemy soldier, was here by his side. "What about you, Wes, you ever hear from your sisters back home?"

Jack watched the emotions play across Wesley's face, or what he could see of it. Wesley wore a beard that hung down several inches longer than Jack's stubble, and his hair, now that he wasn't wearing a cap, hid most of the rest. But his eyes were still expressive, darting from Jack's face to those in the surrounding beds, as if afraid they might betray a deeply hidden secret. A breath of resignation escaped his lungs, and Jack watched as Wesley's shoulders dropped. Leaning forward, elbows on knees, he shook his head. "Haven't heard from anyone for two years now. And I stopped writing, oh, I don't know, a long time ago. No way to get mail through, ya know."

Jack could hear the pain behind the words, could see it in his friends face. "I hear from Jennie a lot, too. She told me she runs into Julia and Annie once in a while."

Wesley's whole demeanor changed at the mention of is sister's names. He sat up straighter, and his eyes lit up in anticipation of good things to come. "Really? How did they look? How did they fare?"

A sudden pain shot through Jack's arm. He flinched involuntarily, putting a quick halt to anything further Wesley might have said. When it passed, he forced a smile, knowing Wesley was waiting with bated breath for any news of his family back home. "She says they're doing just fine. They have money problems just like everyone else in town, but they're getting by. They miss you, I'll tell you that much, and they live for this blasted war to be over, just like the rest of us. They'd really love to see you again, Wes."

Wesley, the stoic, battle scared, march hardened, Confederate soldier bit his bottom lip to keep control of his emotions and eyes from glistening over too much. "Yeah, me too," was all he could say.

An uncomfortable silence grew between the two friends. Wesley folded and unfolded his hands, playing a mindless game with his entwining fingers. Jack went back to staring at the 'map of Gettysburg' on the wall.

Jack broke the silence first. "You ever think much about Heaven?"

Wesley stopped fidgeting with his hands. "All the time."

"Me too."

There was another moment of silence until Wesley found his tongue. "Old Jack, that's what we called old Stonewall while he was still with us, made it a rule that everyone had to attend Sunday services even when we were on the march." He gave a sort of snort, but there was a smile on his face. "That old man was something else, I tell you. He could fight like a cock rooster every day of the week, but 'Sunday belonged to The Lord,' he always said, and wanted the rest of us to worship right along with him. Course, there were some Sunday's when that wasn't possible, what with the war and all, but he always tried his best to make it work out. He's gone now, too, but I expect you know that."

Jack nodded his head. He had heard about the ambush and death of the famous Stonewall Jackson by his own men about a month ago.

"Anyway, I always made sure I went to services, even if they were only held around a camp fire someplace. I was there once when old Jack led them himself. I tell you, that man really knew his stuff. You could walk away from one of those meetings knowing full well that you were either gong to end this war and march home to Gettysburg or Heaven, one or the other, and it didn't matter which."

"I tell you, Wes, I don't think I'm going to see Gettysburg ever again, nor any of my family or Jennie again."

"Don't say that, Jack. You'll be up and moving around again in no time, you'll see."

Jack shook his head. "That's not true, not this time. I can feel it. I don't think I'm going to get out of this hospital. And even if I do, it will only be to end up in some prison someplace, and we both have heard the stories that come out of there." Jack looked up into Wesley's eyes then, his look conveying that he didn't hold him personally responsible for what happened or whatever was to come.

But Wesley felt the weight of unsaid words, and time spent mindlessly marching when it could have been spent in prayer. Time, the one commodity that cannot be stored away, saved up, mended and used on another day. But it did offer us memories, memories that could be retrieved at a moments notice, triggered by a sound, a look in someone's face, an aroma in the air, the touch of someone's hand, or the whisper of a prayer.

Wesley looked hard at Jack, the wounded enemy soldier, and this man he called friend. Beads of perspiration appeared, ringing his hairline now, and his face was taking on a pink hue, the first signs of fever. But his eyes were still clear and alert. "Jack, listen to me. I have to leave just now, need to report back for duty, but I'll be back. I'll be back as quickly as I can so we can talk some more." Leaning forward conspiratorially, Wesley whispered, "I'm sorry I didn't go back to Gettysburg with the others when this war broke out, Jack. If I had I might have been wearing blue like you, been by your side throughout it all, and maybe you wouldn't be lying here now, all broken up this way."

"Don't say that, Wes. Everything that has happened is part of God's plan, and neither you nor me can change that. We can't even *know* it! All we can do is be content with what He gives us, and be thankful for His Grace and Mercy. You couldn't have stopped that bullet that was meant for me any more than you could have stopped this war from coming. But you're a terrific friend for saying so, and I'll never forget it."

Wesley didn't trust his voice for further conversation. He carefully leaned down and took Jack's good hand between his two, giving him a weak smile at the same time. "I'll be back later tonight," he said, and quickly left the room.

True to his word, Wesley came back for his visit with Jack shortly after supper was served. There was still plenty of daylight left, the air still warmed from the heat of the sun. There were two windows in the room where Jack and the other wounded prisoners lie, both of them open to allow any breeze that chanced to enter. There were still six men in Jack's room, but one of them was a new fellow, the other probably having succumbed to his wound. Wesley found Jack barely awake, his eyes fighting to stay open as he approached his cot. To Wesley's sorrow, the fever that was threatening Jack earlier now had a sure stronghold. Wesley reclaimed the single chair in the room that had found its way back into the corner. He sat it down next to Jack's cot. "Hey," he said, "I have news. Looks like we're about to be heading north in another day or so, maybe all the way into Pennsylvania. As much as I hate to say it, I hope we get close enough to Gettysburg for me to sneak off for a visit."

The smile of greeting slowly left Jack's face. "Yeah, I heard the same thing. The nurses that come in here are quick to point out who's going north and who is probably headed farther south, if you know what I mean."

"I do, and they don't have any call to be talking that way. They're just a bunch of ne'er do well's, that's all. Don't listen to them Jack, don't! I just know that everything is going to work out for the best. I can feel it in my bones. God didn't let us meet up this way for nothing, not after all these years."

"No, He didn't, my friend. I have to say, I have mixed feelings about you boys heading north, especially if you're marching into Pennsylvania, or anywhere close to Gettysburg. It's going to be hell on those people if you get anywhere close to that town. Jennie told me not too long ago about a cavalry unit that got as close as Cashtown and Chambersburg. It scared the people to death and I wouldn't want that to happen to them again, no, sir! On the other hand, I think it would be wonderful if you could somehow get home for a visit to see Julia and Annie for awhile.

"I know. I've had the same thoughts."

"If you do get close enough, do you think you could do me a favor?"

"Anything, Jack, just name it." Wesley sat up straighter in his chair, eager at the prospect of doing something for his friend.

Jack reached his hand beneath his blanket and brought out a folded letter. "I worked on this all afternoon while you were gone, hoping you'd come back and do this favor for me."

"I told you, Jack, I'll do anything. What is it?"

Jack seemed to hesitate for a moment, the words getting caught in his throat. "It's a letter, for Jennie. Do you think you could get it through the lines to her?" As he spoke, he handed the folded piece of paper into Wesley's hand.

Wesley accepted it like the treasure it was, and slipped it inside his jacket pocket. "God willing, I'll deliver it in person. How will that be?"

"I'd like that very much."

The two friends were silent for several minutes, each lost in their own thoughts. Someone stuck their head in the door, looking for Wesley. "Oh, there you are! Better get going, Wes, the captain is looking for you."

"Be right there," Wesley called over his shoulder.

Reaching down for Jack's hand, he gave it a long squeeze. "I'm sorry, but it looks like I have to get going. I'm sure glad for the time we had to get caught up again after all these years." He patted the pocket where he had placed the letter. "And don't worry about this either. I'll see that Jennie gets it, one way or the other. And one way or another, we will meet again, Jack. If not on this side of Heaven, then the other, either way, I look forward to it."

"Me, too, Wes, me too."

And with that, Wesley got to his feet and strode to the door without looking back. Jack stared at the empty doorway for a few seconds, the finality of their parting hanging like a heavy weight on his heart. Turning his head, his eyes sought the spider crack on the wall, the one that reminded him of a street map of Gettysburg. The fever seemed to be coming on quicker now, hot, consuming, like a forest fire out of control. Funny, he thought, how the pain in his shoulder had gone from sharp to a dull ache, to nonexistent. His eyelids got heavy, and finally he decided not to fight its weight any longer. He closed them, and yet that map of Gettysburg, of home, was etched into his brain. He stared at it all the harder, letting it call him home. And suddenly there was a face amidst the map. At first he thought it was Jennie, Jennie with long brown hair hanging down to her shoulders, but then he realized that he had never seen Jennie with her hair hanging loose like that before. His breathing quickened at the sight of her, then slowed when he realized it wasn't Jennie at all, but Jesus. Jesus, who was coming to take him home. Not to his home in Gettysburg, but his home in Heaven. His heart rate quickened in anticipation, but then slowed in the wonder of it all. Jesus reached down his hand toward Jack, and Jack reached up both of his towards His Savior – *both* of his! The pain was gone, all of it, and nothing remained but a glorious feeling of coming home.

Chapter 5

Gettysburg

Monday, June 23, 1863

"Be content with such things as you have.
For He Himself has said,
"I will never leave you nor forsake you."
Hebrews 13:5

"Well, that ought to do it. If I need anything else, I'll send for it." Mrs. Wade fastened the buckle on her carpetbag, tucking one more article, an extra hankie, into a side pocket. "John, will you carry this over to your sister's house for me, please?" She stepped away from the bed, allowing John access to the bag, and followed him out of the room. Jennie had been standing in the doorway, watching the proceedings.

Mrs. Wade patted her daughter's cheek as she walked past, down the stairs and towards the front door. "Are you sure you're going to be alright here alone, dear?"

"Of course, Mama. The boys and I will be just fine. It's George that needs you now more than ever. I just wish I could be there too, that's all." Jennie shrugged her shoulders slightly and gave a petulant pout. She knew the words sounded selfish, even to her own ears. But her sister was about to have her first baby, the first baby in the family since Harry came along, and she wanted to be a part of it.

Mrs. Wade reached up to pat Jennie's cheek one more time. "My dear child, Georgia knows, and I know how much you would like to be there, but you have seen her house, you know how tiny it is. Where would everyone sleep? And who's to say how long it might take for this babe to come into the world? It's her first, and first's sometimes take their gay time about making an entrance. No, you'd be better served to wait here and take care of the house and boys until I call for you. I promise to send word as soon as possible after the babe is born."

Mrs. Wade turned her attention from her daughter to her son, standing impatiently at the front door, hand on the knob. "As far as this other nonsense is concerned," she began.

"It isn't nonsense, Mama. You've read the articles in the paper yourself. You've heard that the whole Rebel army is on it's way north, why they were just in Chambersburg the other day, and might this very minute be on their way to our very town!"

"Lower your voice please! Do you want to frighten the wits out of the children?"

"Course not, but I have to get a move on. I talked to that cavalry recruiter and he's expecting me to come and sign up today and I want to get at it, so can we please get going now?"

Mrs. Wade turned her attention back to Jennie. "Don't listen to him. You'll be fine, just stay in the house, and remember, I'm only just down the street, so come and get me if you need me. All right?"

"We'll be fine, Mama." Jennie gave her mother a kiss, then stood aside as she kissed Harry and hugged Isaac. Within a few minutes she was out the door, and silence descended on the house like the calm before a storm. When she turned around she saw Harry standing there, her Bible in his outstretched hands. "It's time to read now, Jennie. Right?"

Was there ever a sweeter child, Jennie wondered as she accepted the proffered book and made her way to the rocking chair in the corner. Both boys sat patiently on the floor, waiting for Jennie to begin the day's devotional reading. Jennie opened to The Book of Psalms, knowing it was the boys' favorite. "Let's see, Psalm 59, verse 16: 'But I will sing of thy power; yea, I will sing aloud of thy mercy in the morning: for thou hast been my defense and refuge in the day of my trouble'."

Chapter 6

Gettysburg

Friday, June 26, 1863

"And whatever you do, whether in word or deed,
do it all in the name of The Lord Jesus,
giving thanks to God the Father through Him."
Colossians 3:17

Jennie, Harry, and Isaac were in the garden weeding, though Jennie was doing most of the real work. The barefoot boys, in an effort to merge playtime with work, were seeing who could pick the most weeds with their toes. Harry was winning, and getting dirtier in the bargain. Jennie reveled in their giggles and occasional burst of laughter, lost in the memory of another warm day, much like this one, when Jack came to tell her good-bye. It seemed like ages ago since she had seen his face, felt his arms around her, or heard his voice. Three months he had said. Three months was all they needed to "teach those Southern boys a lesson they won't soon forget" and come back home. Well, three short months has now turned into three long years , and Jennie couldn't help but think that if this is the way the army does its calculations, she is glad they don't have any say in how long a woman would carry a baby before delivery!

Glancing over at the boys she noticed that Isaac was losing the battle for the pile of most weeds. Making her way to their end of the row, she deftly tried adding some of her own weeds to Isaac's pile. Putting her finger to her lips, she warned him into silence. He acknowledged her with a crooked grin, so she quietly added a few more. But on her third attempt Harry caught her in the act.

"Hey! That's cheating!" Harry jumped to his feet in a flash, catching Jennie by surprise. She screamed in mock horror and made a dash for the house. Harry was right behind her. She was halfway up the back porch steps when the door opened, her brother John standing in the doorway. Jennie couldn't stop in time, and plowed right into him. Harry, so close on her heels added to the forward impetus, the force of which knocked them all onto the ground in a heap.

Harry squealed in delight, buried as he was in the many folds of Jennie's skirt. Isaac's laughter followed them all into the house. But John was livid.

"Now, look what you've done! You got my brand new uniform all over the dirty floor!" It was then that Jennie realized he had been holding a neatly folded blue wool uniform of a cavalry soldier in his arms when she collided so abruptly with him. Getting to his feet, he gave her a hand up before bending down to retrieve his now crumpled uniform and place it on the table.

Once calm had been restored and young Isaac brought back inside, John turned to Jennie. She was standing in the kitchen, holding up the uniform sack coat for inspection. "It doesn't look any the worse for wear," she commented.

John grabbed the trousers and held them up against his waist, letting the legs fall to the ground. "Well, maybe not. But look how big this thing is! I'm supposed to report for duty today and this here uniform is more than two sizes too big. Do you think you could fix it for me, Jen?"

"Of course, I can, but it's going to take a bit of time. I'll tell you what, you go and try it on so I can get it pinned just right, and while I'm working on fixing it you can run to

Fahnestock's and pick up some floor, sugar, and salt that we need for the pantry. It will save me the chore of trying to do it later today, all right?"

"I guess. But that sounds a lot like woman's work to me and I wouldn't want the other fellows to see me doing any such thing."

"You're right, of course. Here, give me that list. I'll go to Fahnestock's and you can wear this uniform just as it is. I'm sure it will be just fine, and they won't make any more fun of you than they would if they were to see you doing something to help out your family in need."

"Oh, never mind! I'll go to Fahnestock's this one last time, but from now on you'll need to look at me like the Union soldier that I am and treat me accordingly. As of today I am the official bugler of the Twenty-first Pennsylvania Cavalry Regiment, Company B. You understand?" John stood up straighter, revealing his full height of five feet-three inches, and proudly puffed out his chest.

Jennie rolled her eyes. "Oh, posh! You'll run to the market if I ask you to. I can't alter your uniform, take care of the boys and the house, and keep up with the tailor shop all by myself. Mama has been up at Georgia's house for days now already, and who knows when she might have that baby and Mama can come back home?"

Jennie tossed the uniform in her brother's direction. "Now here! Hurry up and try this on so I can get it pinned and get busy on the alterations."

It was close to noon when Jennie finished all of the alterations. John proudly modeled his new uniform, strutting through the tailor shop, into the kitchen, and back again. "What do you think, Jen? How does it look?"

Jennie couldn't believe the transformation, how simply donning a blue wool uniform could change a boy into a man with no more effort than that. Though she had to begrudgingly admit that at seventeen he could hardly be considered a mere boy any longer. "It looks right smart on you, John, if I do say so myself."

John's smile grew still larger on his face, as he beamed in her praise and that of the boys. Reaching for his kepi, he adjusted it on his head, and glanced at himself in the mirror for the first time. "I do look right smart, don't I?" His smile brought out the teasing in his words, bringing guffaws from the others in the room. He accepted the bantering as his due for a few moments and then headed for the door. "Well, I'd best be getting on. The boys will be waiting for me."

"Don't forget to stop by and say good-bye to Mama before you leave town now." Jennie got up to give her brother a hug, all the while fighting to dispel the image of Jack standing just as proud before he marched out of town with his own unit, oh, so long ago. The hug lasted longer than usual, broken by the loud, exaggerated coughing from Harry.

"Oh, yes, sorry." Jennie broke away from her brother, reaching for a hankie at the same time. When at last John was ready to leave, Jennie and Harry followed him onto the porch, watched him mount his horse, and ride off down the street. John waved a final wave as he disappeared around the corner, swallowed up in a cloud of dust and pounding hooves.

Harry went back inside the house long before Jennie, who stayed on the porch until the last particle of dust settled back down on the street. She was tired of the leave takings, of the saying good-byes. So many of her friends, full of patriotism and good intentions, had waved the same such happy good-bye, never to be seen again. It's true that some were still out there, somewhere, fighting with their units. But there were others, too many others, who were even now buried in faraway places, never to be seen this side of Heaven again. Immediately, and as always, her thoughts turned to Jack. Sometimes, surrounded as they were with the constant reminders of war, it was hard to think of anything else. Jack was in every blue uniform, every spring-like day, the caress of a cool breeze teasing her hair, the words to a hymn, and the laughter of gentlemen she passed on the street.

Tears were welling up in her eyes when she heard the sound of someone screaming her name. Lost in thoughts of Jack, it took a moment for the urgency in the scream to sink in. Looking up, she saw Maria, their dear friend, running down the street, waving her arms to get Jennie's attention.

"Jennie! Jennie! George just gave birth to a baby boy! Isn't that wonderful?"

Jennie ran down the porch steps and into Maria's outstretched arms. Laughing and crying, they hugged again and again. "You are officially an aunt now, my dear!"

Filled with excitement, Jennie could hardly find her voice. "Oh, Aunt Jennie. That does sound good, doesn't it? But is George all right? Is the baby all right? How is Mama? Tell me everything!" The two women went inside the house to talk about the birth of a baby, rather than the leave-taking of another family member. It was going to be a joyous day after all!

An hour later the smiles faded from their faces when Harry came bounding up the back porch steps and into the kitchen. Quite out of breath, they could hardly make out his words.

"There's....sold.....soldiers.....coming....into....town.... the.....diamond..."

"That's enough, Harry. Now calm down, start over, and tell me again what has happened." Jennie set her teacup down on the table, her focus now on her little brother's revelation. Harry held onto the side of the table for support, drawing in great gulps of air. Outside, the sound of rising turmoil filled the street, racing in through the open windows like hornets disturbed from their nest.

"What is going on?"

"That's what I been trying to tell you! The Rebel army is back, I seen 'm myself down in the diamond, and there are a lot of them, too!"

Both women were on their feet in an instant.

"Well, if that's true, then I'd best be getting back home. Henry will be wondering what happened to me anyway, and we're going to have a lot to do if those devils are back again. Good-bye Jennie, you take care of yourself now."

Jennie followed her friend to the door, gazing into the street and seeing the commotion for herself. Not for the first time did she see townspeople rushing madly through the streets, some purposefully and others in near hysteria, some empty handed and others weighted down with bundles.

Mr. Rupp, the tanner from down the street, was rushing by when Jennie called out to him. "Is it true then? Have the Rebel soldiers come back?"

Mr. Rupp slowed down but did not stop. "Yes, I'm afraid they have. The whole Confederate army is about to march into town any minute now! Some of them are congregating down in the diamond this very minute, and if you'll pardon me I have to get back to my shop before they get there first. Mischief follows that army wherever they go!"

Others were screaming the same thing.

"Lock your shutters and doors!"

"Come along, Emil, I have to get that silver hidden from sight!"

"This is too much, just too much! To think they're coming back again!"

And on it went, as one after another ran past the house to the safety of their own homes.

The day was turning out to be a hot one, the sun beating down unmercifully. Jennie reached for her bonnet on a peg by the door. "I have to go and see what's going on, Harry, I simply have to. You and Isaac stay here in the house. Lock both of the doors, and don't open them for anyone, you understand? I will be back just as soon as I can." And with that, she walked out the door, calling from the other side. "Now lock this door tight, Harry!"

Jennie waited until she heard the latch turning on the other side before rushing down the steps into the street. The commotion was bigger, busier on Baltimore Street, than on the less traveled Breckenridge Street where she lived, so she turned in that direction. Various degrees of panic or determination were on everyone's face. Drivers yelled at inattentive pedestrians running into their path, and horses screamed when brought up short. The negroes in particular were panic stricken, and who could blame them? With bundles on their backs and stuffed satchels in their hands, they hurried down the street as if Beezlebub himself were chasing them, as indeed, he just might be.

The dust from so many people milling about, and horses and wagons rushing by, got into Jennie's eyes and throat, coating her bonnet and dress. Squinting through the haze she searched for some familiar face to make inquiries of. Finally she spotted Mr. Pierce standing in front of his butcher shop. He was saddling a horse, and helping her brother, Samuel, to mount.

She had to call him several times before he heard her over the din. "Mr. Pierce! Mr. Pierce! What are you doing? What's going on?"

Before he could reply, Samuel excitedly called out. "I'm taking Washington here out of town to safety. The Rebels are on their way to Gettysburg Jennie, can you believe it?" Samuel reached down to pat the neck of Washington, the Pierces' newest and favorite horse.

There was none of the hysteria in Mr. Pierces' face, yet his actions as he loaded a bulging saddlebag onto the back of his horse showed plainly that he wasn't unfamiliar with what was going on.

"It's true then?" Jennie turned her pleading eyes on Mr. Pierce.

"I'm afraid so, dear, and we haven't much time. Young Samuel here is going to take Washington to my brother's farm outside of town. They'll both be safe there until our own soldiers arrive and chase these Rebels back down south where they came from. And good riddance to them, I say!"

"But isn't it dangerous sending a young boy on such a mission? Samuel is only twelve years old, Mr. Pierce!"

Finished ministering with the saddlebags, Mr. Pierce slapped the rump of his horse, sending Samuel racing down the street out of town. Wrapped up in the excitement and adventure of the moment, Samuel looked over his shoulder, smiling and waving his hat at his sister.

"He will be fine Jennie. I have known and treated that boy as if he were my own son for years now. He'll ride Washington to my brother's house and stay there until I send word for him to return. Now you best get back home yourself, young lady. Word is that hundreds of enemy soldiers are on the march from York and coming down that very pike this very minute. There is no time to lose! Now run along and take care of things at home, I still have much to do myself."

Mr. Pierce disappeared inside his house, leaving Jennie standing on the boardwalk, wringing the hankie in her hands. People continued racing by, several bumping her as they did. Reluctantly, Jennie turned back towards home. There was nothing she could do about Samuel now, but Harry and Isaac would still certainly need her attention. With each step she took a sense of urgency increased her speed. The sound of slamming shutters followed her, each one making its own clapping sound, like the audience at the beginning of a play waiting for the action to start. She had just made it to the first step of her front porch when several shots rang out. They were followed immediately by screams, and Jennie was torn between dashing inside the house and the desire to run back to the corner to see what had happened. The decision was taken from her when the sound of racing horses brought her up short, along with several more shots, closer this time. It was from behind her on Baltimore Street, and when she turned in their direction fear, the likes of which she had never known, froze her in place.

Half a dozen horses or more, carrying soldiers in grey uniforms, were brandishing pistols and racing determinedly down the street, away from the diamond. Harry opened the door at the sound of gunshots, his voice pleading for Jennie to hurry inside. Wonderful as that sounded, hiding away from the chaos and calamity on the street, curiosity got the better of her. Turning back towards Baltimore Street, she called over her shoulder. "Keep that door closed tight, Harry. I'll only be a minute more. I simply must see what's going on."

She heard the sound of the door close as she made her way back to the corner. To her surprise the horses that had been racing out of town only moments before were now heading back up the street towards the diamond. The enemy soldiers glanced in her direction, but seeing no threat, turned their attention elsewhere. She couldn't believe how dirty and unkempt they all appeared. Their uniforms, if you could call them that, seemed put together piecemeal. None of them wore the same style of hat, each seeming to choose whatever suited them best, and the color of their clothing was not only grey, but butternut tan, and even shades of faded blue, as if they had stolen it from Union soldiers. All of the breath left her lungs as she contemplated what that could mean. But before she could dwell on it further she heard her name called from amidst the group of riders. Squinting to see through the dust, she was horrified to see Samuel still astride Washington. He was holding onto the pommel of the saddle while one of the Rebel soldiers had hold of the reins.

"Jennie!" Samuel called again. "Help me!"

"Shut it, boy!" Another of the soldiers threatened Samuel with the back of his pistol, but didn't actually strike him.

Jennie's hand flew to her mouth, but the scream had already escaped. Without a second thought she darted into the street, pleading with the soldiers who held her brother. "Please! What are you going to do with him? Can't you see he's just a child? Let him go!"

"Cain't do that, miss," was the only response she received. The rest of her entreaties went unanswered. Their pace had slowed to a trot, and though Jennie was not able to keep pace with them, she was at least able to follow the group of riders and her brother. Looking ahead to the diamond, she could see at least a hundred more of the unkempt soldiers in grey milling about. There were townspeople amidst them as well, most of who seemed to be pleading with them over one thing or another, the same way she was over her brother.

Jennie reached the diamond in time to see Samuel being roughly dragged from Washington. He was hauled before another soldier, who Jennie took to be the one in charge. She couldn't hear what was being said over the din of chatter and shouts surrounding her. Determined to free her brother, she marched towards that smaller group of soldiers. Suddenly, her path was barred by an equally determined soldier. His musket was held in both hands diagonally across his chest, and he used it as a means of stopping her progress without actually touching her.

"Sorry, miss, but that's as far as you git."

"But that's my brother! What are you doing with him?"

"Ain't up for me to say. The General Early hisself will decide that."

Jennie made a move to get around him, but he blocked her every step. Over his shoulder she could see the general talking with some of his men. To her mind he was not that impressive looking. Standing of average height and build, he sported a shaggy beard like most of those surrounding him, and his clothes were only slightly less crumpled looking.

Tired now of "dancing" with the guard, she gave him her most fierce scowl, and fought her way back through the crowd. Her last look was of Samuel standing with several others regarded as prisoners up against the Wills' house.

Hurrying back down Baltimore Street, Jennie pondered what to do. The streets were thinning of traffic now, with only a few of the more curious making their way towards the diamond in the center of town, the better to see what was going on. Most people chose to peer from behind closed doors and curtains.

Up until the moment she reached the corner of Breckenridge Street Jennie hadn't known what she should do. Samuel was in dire straights, but she had been denied access to the General Early, the one who apparently controlled her brother's fate. Sending up a quick prayer for help and guidance, Jennie was amazed as her feet seemed to move of their own volition past her corner and on down Baltimore Street towards Georgia's house. Suddenly it occurred to her that she must get word to her mother. Yes, her mother would know what to do. Surely no soldiers could turn away the mother of a child the way they did a young woman, a mere sister.

A few minutes later Jennie was rushing to the back door of her sister's home. It was a red brick home, a dual family home actually. Georgia and Louis lived in the northern half of the building, while the McClain family lived in the other half. Jennie didn't bother to knock, but let herself inside the house. Stepping into the kitchen, she spotted her sister sleeping on the bed in the front parlor, the newborn baby swaddled and sleeping beside her. It took all of her willpower not to run across the room, grab that little baby up, smell the wonder of him, and pretend that the rest of the world didn't exist. But their mother was sitting in a rocking chair near the window, knitting, her eyebrows creased in a slight frown. Before Jennie could utter a word, her mother held a finger to her lips for silence.

Out of breath now, Jennie waved her mother over, nodding towards the open door behind her at the same time.

Mrs. Wade plopped the knitting in a basket beside her chair and tiptoed across the room. "Something's wrong. What is it? Tell me you didn't leave Harry and Isaac alone just so you could come and see our newest addition."

"No, of course not. Oh, Mama, you have to come help. Samuel was taken by those Rebel soldiers and is being held like a prisoner down on the diamond. I tried to make them let him go but they wouldn't listen to me."

"What are you talking about? What Rebel soldiers?" Mrs. Wade's face held a look of complete puzzlement.

"Mama, didn't you hear the shots, or all of the commotion in the street earlier?"

Mrs. Wade shook her head. "Why, no. It must have all happened while I was trying to start a fire in the stove. Shoving all of that wood around makes such a racket, you know, I didn't hear a thing." But she took the time to look around now, noticing the streets devoid of traffic, and the odd silence that hung in the air as if the whole town was holding its breath, waiting to see what would happen next.

"Please, Mama, his name is General Early, the man they said who would decide Samuel's fate. You must hurry and see what you can do. I'll stay here with Georgia in case she wakes up and needs anything."

Mrs. Wade went inside the house long enough to retrieve her bonnet before rushing off on an errand to save her young son.

When she arrived at the diamond she found it congested with soldiers and townspeople alike, though women in attendance were definitely in the minority. Her eyes searched everywhere for Samuel, but he was nowhere to be seen. Then, not knowing what else to do, she began asking any of the numerous soldiers milling about, how to locate her son. The distress on her face clearly evident, a young Confederate soldier finally took pity on her and led her to General Early.

"Sir, sir, you're holding my young son, Samuel Wade, and they tell me that you are the only one who can release him. He's only twelve years old and has done nothing wrong. Please have pity on this old mother and let me take him home with me.
"

The general looked at Mrs. Wade, bewildered. Leaning towards one of his aides, he listened to what he had to say.

"The boy was caught leaving town on a horse, sir. We apprehended him and brought him here." The aide pointed in he direction of the other prisoners herded against the side of the Wills' house.

"Was he wearing a uniform at the time?"

"No, sir, he was not. We are treating him as a spy."

Mrs. Wade's hand flew to her mouth, stifling a scream of shock.

"Twelve years old, you say?"

Mrs. Wade finally found her tongue. "Yes, general, only twelve years old, a mere boy. And not much good to anyone but his own dear mother."

"I see."

There was silence for a moment while General Early digested this bit of information. He asked only one other question of his aide. "And where is the horse now?"

"Tethered with the others, sir, and being taken back to the trains."

"Well, then, madam, since this boy of yours is of no value to us or to anyone else, according to you, I will release him into your custody. But the horse stays with us. Perhaps you should consider teaching him a trade of some sort, make him an asset to the community one day. Now, if you will excuse me, I have much more business to transact. That will be all."

Mrs. Wade barely had a chance to offer thanks before being led away by one of the general's aides. He took her over to Samuel, gained his release, and sent them both on their way.

Samuel, though clearly frightened, was none the worse for wear. Following his mother away from the diamond and the milling soldiers, they spoke not a word until they were several blocks away. It was Samuel who spoke first. "Mr. Pierce is going to kill me when he finds out about Washington."

"He'll do no such thing. Now, the day is getting late, almost time for supper. You get back in there with the Pierces' and learn that trade that will make you an asset to the community one of these days."

Mrs. Wade ushered Samuel into the Pierce household. Mr. Pierce met them both at the door, and though extremely disappointed at the loss of his favorite horse, he was thrilled that Samuel was all right. Leaving the young boy behind, he escorted Mrs. Wade back to Georgia's house and Jennie home to hers rather than have the women out on the streets unescorted with enemy soldiers about.

Chapter 7

Gettysburg

Saturday, June 27, 1863

"This is the day which The Lord hath made;
we will be glad and rejoice in it."
Psalm 118:24

Jennie got very little sleep last night. Though the streets seemed quiet enough, she feared the Rebel soldiers would try something evil, like breaking into the house in search of valuables. It is the one thing the townspeople had heard over and over from citizens in other towns that had been visited by the enemy. The wanton destruction, theft, and ransacking of homes, barns and even chicken coops as the soldiers marched by was something no one wanted to experience. It was even worse when the soldiers spent any amount of time in the town, when they were able to take their time about what homes or buildings they wanted to break into, searching for whatever suited their fancy. She had heard tales of them absconding with rocking chairs, trunks of ladies clothing, bedding, jewelry, silver, jars of preserves, chickens and just about anything else they could tote over their backs.

To make matters worse, she hadn't heard from Jack in – forever! Rising from bed, she reached for the daguerreotype of him that she always kept near. At night it always stood on her dresser, and during the day it was in her apron pocket. Walking towards the window, she tried to see his reflection in the moonlight. Whispering a conversation with him, she struggled to keep her voice low so as not to disturb Harry, asleep in the next room. While she talked she allowed her fingers to stroke his face and the gilt frame that held him captive. "Where are you?" She asked, again and again. "Why don't you write?"

It had been a whole week since the town had heard of a battle in Virginia that some called The Battle of Stephen's Depot and others referred to as The Battle of Carter's Woods. Survivors of the battle, whatever you cared to call it, marched into town, some of them in horrible shape. They had come home to recover from their wounds before rejoining their units. Jennie was not there when they marched down the Chambersburg Pike, but she had heard of it from Jack's mother afterwards. Jennie replayed the conversation in her mind tonight, but it was a tired conversation, one that had been replayed so many times she wanted to put her hands over her ears and make it stop, to go away altogether. *'Jennie, he wasn't with the group. No one had seen him once the battle got underway. It was a terrible rout, with men running in every direction. There was no way to keep track of everyone. No one remembers what happened to Jack, nor who saw him last. One person said he saw him running with Ed, and they were both just fine then. Another said he thought he saw him fall, wounded, but he wasn't sure. There was so much smoke and fusion, mind you, it could have been anybody.'*

Jennie repeated the last five words over and over, like a mantra in her head. *It could have been anybody. It could have been anybody.* It was the only thing that kept her level headed, that kept her sane, the knowledge that Jack *must* still be alive out there somewhere. But why haven't they heard? Why hasn't he written? And the battle would rage in her head again, optimism and pessimism.

At some point during the wee hours, Jennie fell asleep, the haunting battle over Jack's wellbeing finally being laid to rest. When she awoke, his picture was still in her hand, clenched tightly to her breast. The first shades of light were just filtering through the lace curtain at her window, and the sounds of a sleepy village coming alive filtered through. A tremulous smile played the corners of her mouth when Jack's picture was the first thing she saw upon opening her eyes. The remembrance of last night's battle was laid to rest with the singing of the birds and the responsibilities of a new day. Sounds of footsteps could be heard downstairs. The backdoor closed none too quietly. Harry had gone outside to use the necessary and would want his breakfast soon.

Wiping sleep from her eyes, Jennie sat up in bed, still clutching Jack's picture. She looked at him for a long moment, willing him to answer her pleas, to smile back from the frame, to materialize like a vapor and stand before her this very moment. Smiling at her silliness, she closed the cover of the frame and slid it into her pocket. Changing her mind, she retrieved the picture, opened it and gave Jack a quick kiss before closing it one more time. Then, realizing that she was alone in her room and that no one could see her, she kissed him again, longer this time, wantonly, until the sound of Harry knocking on her door brought her up short. Quickly, she snapped the picture frame closed and dropped Jack into her apron pocket. "Coming!"

Her bedroom door emitted its usual loud squeak when opened, and there stood Harry, hair uncombed, shirt hanging half-tucked, and eyes that seemed unsure of whether they even wanted to be open or not. She couldn't help herself, she tussled his hair. "Good morning, little one. Did you sleep well?"

"Not really. I kept thinking of those soldiers and how they wanted to take Samuel away."

"Well I told you that Mama took care of all of that, remember? Samuel is back safe with the Pierce's where he belongs, and there he'll stay. They won't bother him any more now."

"I guess."

The pair had made their way down the stairs and into the kitchen. Jennie opened the window for air, letting the stale, trapped air out and a fresh morning breeze in. Grabbing a skillet from its peg on the wall, she placed it on the cast iron stove. "Why don't you get me some water from the well and a few more logs for the fire. I'll get some breakfast going for us, all right?"

"Sure Jennie. Can we go see the new baby today, do you think?"

"I think that would be a wonderful idea. Maybe we'll do that right after our Bible reading. But we can only stay for a little while. Georgia and her baby still need their rest, and I have a lot of orders to fill today, and I'm sure that a few soldiers in town won't stop some of those people from coming to pick up their mended clothes. Besides, with Mama gone to stay with Georgia I have twice as much work to finish up." Harry hadn't moved from his spot near the open window yet. Turning to him, wooden spoon in hand, Jennie held it threateningly. "I think it's high time I taught you how to thread a needle and do some light mending. What do you say to that?"

"I think I'll go and get that water and wood now."

Harry was out the door in a flash, the door slamming closed behind him. Jennie smiled, then reached into their tiny ice box for the piece of ham she knew was still there. Ham, eggs, and a few biscuits left over from last nights' meal would make for a fine breakfast.

A few minutes later Harry came in, water carelessly dripping on the floor from the water bucket. "Something is going on, Jennie. I heard shouts coming from down the street."

"Where on the street?"

Harry put the bucket down on the floor and pointed towards the north. "That way, towards the diamond."

Jennie unfastened her apron and tossed it quickly over a nearby chair. "Stay right here! I'll be back in a minute, I just want to see what's going on." Retrieving her bonnet from its peg by the door, Jennie went out the front door and hustled down to Baltimore Street. The sounds of cheering reached her ears before she made it around the corner, and this helped her step more lightly. The first person she encountered was Mr. Pierce, with Samuel by his side. "Please, Mr. Pierce, do you know what's happening?"

"Why, yes, dear, we do. It appears the enemy is retreating!" Mr. Pierce chuckled at his own joke, bringing a smile to Jennie's face.

"You mean they're leaving, just like that?"

"Well, not exactly 'just like that.' They have done their fare share of damage and thievery, and threatened people with life and limb, but at least they are leaving town now."

"Oh, that is good news, a wonderful way to start the day, I'd say."

"It would appear so. But there are those that say they could be back this way again when they head back south."

"You mean they're not heading home? Where are they going then?"

"No one is really sure, but I expect we haven't seen the last of those southern soldiers yet. Were I you, I would do what I could to hide my valuables."

Samuel spoke up for the first time since Jennie's arrival. "I'm sorry about Washington, Mr. Pierce."

The gentleman put his hand on Samuel's shoulder. "I know you are, boy, we've talked about this before. You only did what you could and no more. Nothing that happened was your fault and if you bring it up again, well, I'm afraid I might just have to box your ears." The smile on his face belied the mischief in his eyes, and both brother and sister smiled.

Others were now gathering in the street, wishing a good morning, and sharing stories of personal encounters with the enemy soldiers. All were thrilled that they had left more quietly than they had arrived.

Her friend, Maria, was standing on the boardwalk with her husband, Henry, as Jennie turned for home. "Isn't it wonderful Jennie? Those horrid soldiers are gone now and things can get back to normal around here. "

"It is good news indeed. Thanks be to God!"

"What news do you hear from Georgia? I heard she had her baby yesterday, a little boy, I believe. Is she all right? I was concerned that this excitement would have caused her some harm. Giving birth is never easy, but one doesn't need enemy soldiers running through the streets adding to the chore."

"That's very true. I'm sure that all is still well, otherwise Mama would have gotten news to me. Harry and I plan on walking down there later this morning to see if we can be of any help, and to see the little fellow for ourselves."

"Oh, it is a glorious day when babies are born, is it not?"

"Simply the best!" They chatted for several more minutes with each other and with neighbors that happened by. From what they could gather it seemed as if most people fared just fine during the occupation. Everyone was concerned for the Sandoe family, who lost their son, George, when the army first marched into town. How tragic, they all agreed, to see your son racing past home, running for his life, and then to see it cut short by enemy fire. Jennie could feel the lump welling in her throat, while others were already reaching for hankies.

"The Lord giveth and The Lord taketh away," someone said.

"Yes, and The Lord also sendeth away," Maria said.

The small group of neighbors chuckled, glad to turn their conversation in a lighter direction.

"Yes, and may that be the last we see of enemy soldiers in Gettysburg!"

"Amen!" They all agreed.

As Jennie walked away Maria called after her. "Tell Georgia to rest easy now. The Rebel devils are gone and won't be back to bother us again! That ought to help her to sleep."

*　　　　　*　　　　　*　　　　　*
*

Wesley Culp was in his marching trance again. One foot in front of the other, not losing sight of the man's heel in marching in front of him. He had no idea where they were, only that someone had said they passed into Pennsylvania several miles back. He glanced up at that, searching for familiar landmarks, anything that would indicate they were getting closer to home, but seeing none, he went back to his semi-sleeping marching stance. It was hard to explain to those who had never had to march for miles in all kinds of weather, just what it was like to sleep standing up and moving forward at the same time. He tried to explain it to an artilleryman once, one of those who rode on the wagon most of the time, but he simply did not get it. In the end he decided it was a gift, a talent given them by Old Stonewall hisself, who used to fall asleep in the saddle they say, just like his men did on the march. Many were the times they would joke about it around the campfire at night. What if the lead unit fell asleep and walked off a cliff or something? There would go the whole Rebel army!

"What are you snickering about?" Ned, his marching buddy these past few days, glanced at Wesley curiously. The two were similar in stature and disposition, but where Wesley

152

was dark haired, Ned was blonde. Born in Virginia not too far from Shepherdstown, where Wesley had lived these past several years, it was only natural that they would eventually meet up and become friends.

Wesley looked up in surprise. He hadn't realized that he had laughed out loud. But seeing the look on Ned's face he couldn't help himself, he chuckled again. "I was just thinking how blindly we march to and fro all over creation without ever asking why or even where we're going. We could march right off the side of a cliff and into the ocean before anyone might come to their senses, if then!"

"Those are true words, my boy. But do you want to be the one who walks up to the general and say, 'scuze me, sir, but me and the boys were jest wonderin' why we're marching down this road today, and where zactly does it lead?" Ned exaggerated his southern accent, making his dialog more comical, and they both had to chuckle at their wit.

Too soon though, they realized they were wasting valuable breath and energy. They quieted, resorting to putting one foot in front of the other, and following the fellow in front of them.

That night, while sitting around the campfire, Wesley, Ned, Ben and others from their unit brought up the conversation again. "So, Wes, we're in Pennsylvania now, ain't that where you're from?"

"Yeah, a long time ago." Wesley stared into the empty cup in his hands. They had real coffee for a change, bought and paid for with Confederate scrip from some farmhouse along the way, and it went down real quick. The trouble was, the real coffee, so long omitted from his diet, made him think all the more of home, and not his home in Shepherdstown either, but home in Gettysburg. He had to admit that he didn't really recognize the lay of the land yet, but it was almost like a sense of "home" surrounding him with each step he took of late. The ground felt just as hard beneath his sore feet, and the pines, maples, oaks and wild apple trees all looked similar to those around his adopted home of Shepherdstown, yet there was something so familiar to the countryside they had been marching through. Familiar, and yet different somehow, as if the very land itself was saying 'you don't belong any more, you're not one of us.'

"Wes, you're awful quiet there. Ain't you a gonna answer Ned's question? He done asked you twice already."

Wesley looked up. "Oh, sorry Ben, just tired from the march, I guess. What did you want to know Ned?"

"I said I heard tell we was gonna march all the way to the state capitol, which I thought I heard 'em say was Harrisburg. Your town anywhere close to that?"

Wesley shook his head. "Not really. Gettysburg, where I'm from, is a hard days ride south of there. It ain't likely we'll get anywhere close to that tiny town if Harrisburg is where we're headed."

"Gettysburg." Ned said the word softly, thoughtfully. "Seems to me I heard tell along the march that we jest might march straight through that town. I forget who said it, but I recollect hearing that name awhile back. Something about meeting up with the cav boys there, or Longstreet, or some such thing."

Ben slapped Wesley on the back. "How 'bout that? You might make it back to your hometown before any of the rest of us! Wouldn't that be something?"

Wesley forced a chuckle. "Yeah, really something." Rising to his feet, Wesley moved away from the fire, looking for a place to settle down for the night.

"Hey, Wes, you gonna try and see your family if we get close enough to Gettysburg, ain't ya," Ned called after him, but Wesley ignored the question, waving a hand goodnight as he stepped farther away from the fire. When his eyes adjusted to the darkness he discovered a tree with only one other soldier leaning up against it. He didn't recognize the fellow by name, so knew it would be a safe bet the fellow wouldn't know about his northern heritage or his birth in Gettysburg. A smile and a nod, and Wesley claimed the opposite side of the tree for himself. Jacks letter to Jennie crinkled in his pocket as he sat down, reminding him of his promise to deliver it if they get close enough to town. Wesley's heart started beating faster at the very thought of home now, but there was fear wrapped up in that excitement. Fear of what he might have to do, who he might have to shoot in his own hometown, fear of what they might do to him if they recognize him for who he is. He almost chuckled at that notion, however. There is no way anyone but family would recognize him now, and even family might be stretching it a bit. Wesley glanced down at his bare feet, dirty, cracked, and bleeding in parts. His clothes were worn through in so many places that even the patches had patches sewn onto them. He was thinner than when he left, with a much shaggier beard and longer hair. No, he wouldn't have anything to fear regarding being recognized.

The more he thought about his own appearance, the more he was determined to visit his own sisters, to see how much they might have changed since he left home. Julia and Annie were probably the only ones in town who would recognize him as things stood right now. Well, they and maybe Jennie. Yes, Jennie might see the resemblance to what he used to be, they had been so close after all. Patting the letter from Jack and remembering his promise, Wesley knew without a doubt that he would have to figure out a way to get into town for a quick visit no matter what. That is if they did indeed get close enough for him to sneak away, if only for a little while. And if he got into town to deliver this missive to a friend, he might just as well take the time to say hey to his two dear sisters. Who could begrudge him that?

The soldier he was sharing the tree with began snoring softly at first, then louder with each passing breath. Looking back at the fire, Ned and Ben were both prostrate on the ground, their haversacks for a pillow and stars for a blanket. Except for the heat from the fire, which he didn't need on this warm evening, it looked quite inviting. Pushing himself away from the tree, he slowly, with tired limbs, made his way back to his friends. Gettysburg and all of its allure would have to wait until another day.

Chapter 8

Gettysburg

Tuesday, June 30, 1863

"I can do all things through Christ
which strengthenth me."
Philippians 4:13

"Oh, George, he's just the sweetest little boy ever! I could sit here and hold him all day long!" Jennie cradled her tiny nephew, named Louis Kenneth for his father, finally rocking him to sleep with the help of a cool summer breeze through the open window.

"You say that now, but you wouldn't think him so sweet when he cries in the middle of the night for another feeding, or his umpteenth diaper change. His Highness King Louis is quite another story then, believe me." Georgia chuckled at the image of her young son as a member of royalty. Yes, the tiny infant was a lot of work, but he was her tiny infant, and worth all of the labor in the world. She smiled at the sight of her only sister holding him so lovingly, the smile just as bright on both of their faces.

"It's my turn now, isn't it? Don't I get a chance to hold him?" Harry had been sitting on the edge of Georgia's bed, swinging his feet impatiently, and doing his best to be quiet while the adults in the room talked about babies, feedings, laundry, and getting back on ones feet. It was enough to make any eight-year old antsy!

"I only just got him myself, silly! You're just going to have to wait your turn. It's been a long while since I've had the chance to hold one so small and I'm going to relish every minute of it." Jenny leaned down close to the baby, drinking in the sweetness of his clean wrappings, and running a finger lightly down his soft cheek. Strong instincts, the likes of which she didn't know she possessed, took hold. Suddenly she had to fight back tears, wondering if she would ever hold such a precious bundle of her own. A baby created out of love between a man and a woman, between her and Jack. Oh, Jack! Jack, where are you? Why haven't you written?

The baby started to stir, its tiny eyes fluttering open and then closed again. Still Jennie held onto him. Her mother and Georgia had been talking about the close confines of this front parlor, and when would be an appropriate time to return the big bed back upstairs where it rightfully belonged. Several months ago it had been hauled downstairs to save Georgia the many steps up and down during her confinement, but now that the little one was here, perhaps it should be taken out of the way again. It isn't that it was a particularly large bed by any means, but it did have a way of dwarfing the room it inhabited.

Mrs. Wade had the last word on the subject. "We'll give it another day or two, just to make sure you're good on your feet before we call someone in to haul it back upstairs. It was such a chore in the first place, if you remember."

"Yes, I do. For awhile there I thought they were going to have to saw the thing in two to get it around that corner in the stairway. I don't think anyone is overly anxious to go through that again, believe me. Besides, I'm quite comfortable right here." For emphasis, Georgia snuggled down deeper into the bed, pulling a light blanket up to her chin and giggling like a schoolgirl.

Jennie and their mother joined in giggling with her. Mrs. Wade reached over and patted her daughter's hand. "That's right. You just take it easy for a little while, gosh knows you had quite a hard time of it. You deserve a proper rest."

As if aware that the conversation was mainly focused on him, little Louis announced to the world that he was present. Wiggling in Aunt Jennie's arms, he let out a wail that brought everyone in the room up short.

Harry climbed down off of the bed, putting his hands over his ears. "Never mind! I don't want to hold it any more!"

The three women laughed as Harry made his way to the back door, hands still over his ears. Isaac, on a mat in the corner, was doing the same thing.

Reluctantly Jennie got up to return the baby to his mother. "Well, I guess we all know what he wants now, don't we?" Placing the baby in his mother's arms, Jennie said, "well, I guess I'll just swap one bundle for another now and get those boys back home so I can get some work done." Hands on hips, she glanced down at Isaac, a pretend scowl on her face. "Only this bundle is ever so much heavier than tiny Louis over there!"

Isaac merely smiled and held out his arms. He knew there was no bite to her stinging words.

As Jennie juggled Isaac around for a more comfortable grip, her mother called after her. "Which project are you working on today? Did you get those collars tatted for Mrs. Watkins?"

"Yes, Mama, and she has already come and picked them up. I thought I mentioned that to you. She loved them by the

159

way. Today I want to start working on those bodice adjustments for Mrs. Wells. Remember, she got all those hand-me-downs from her sister over in York and needed them all taken in by several inches?"

"Oh, yes, and such pretty dresses, too."

"Most of them were, that's true, but some of them are so old and faded I'm afraid there isn't much material there for the alterations Mrs. Wells needs."

"How many dresses were there anyway?"

"There are seven of them, if you can imagine? Who needs that many dresses anyway? Two of them are in real good shape, suitable for church going and the like, and three others are simple, everyday dresses. The one I like best is that rose-colored tea dress, simply beautiful! I'm not sure about those two black ones though. I'm afraid they might be too faded and thread bare to hold up to any more alterations of any kind."

"Well, you'll have to be very careful then, as I'm sure you will be." Mrs. Wade gave Harry a hug good-bye, then leaned in to hug Jennie and Isaac, tussling his hair at the same time. "You boys play nice now, and let Jennie get some work done, you hear?"

"Yes, Mrs. Wade."

"Yes, Mama, we always do."

"My eye!" Jennie cried in mock indignation. Calling out a good-bye to her sister, Jennie rolled her eyes playfully at her mother before stepping out the door.

When Jennie got the boys home she fed them a quick, light lunch, got them situated, and settled down to work. Readjusting the bodices for Mrs. Wells took Jennie longer than she had thought. Before she knew it her stomach was growling and the boys were clammering for their dinner.

"Please, Jennie, can you stop and fix us something to eat now? We're starving to death in here!"

"Yeah, Miss Jennie. We're starving to death in here!"

"Oh, fuss and nonsense, you're neither of you starving to death!" No sooner had the words left Jennie's mouth than her stomach howled in protest itself. Harry, standing in the doorway, heard it himself. His eyebrows shot upwards, a comical look of surprise on his face. Jennie let the dress bodice she had been working on drop to her lap and covered her stomach with her hands. "But I just might well be! And since it's just as easy to feed two small boys as well as myself I might as well do just that."

Jennie stood, stretched her aching back, and made her way to the kitchen. Reaching for the iron skillet on the way, she let it fall onto the stove with a bang. At that instant the sound of many horses could be heard coming down the street. She turned around, a puzzled look on her face. "Now what's going on," she asked the room in general.

Harry had made it to the window before the words left her mouth. "It's soldiers, Jennie! A lot of them!"

For an instant, fear kept Jennie rooted to the spot. "What color are they wearing?"

"I think they're blue or black, it's kind of hard to tell with all the dust all over everything."

Jennie let out a sigh of relief and hurried to the door to see for herself. Opening it she glanced towards Baltimore Street, where most of the horses seemed to be galloping by. "Oh, thank goodness, they're ours." And just as quickly her relief turned to dismay. If the Union soldiers were here, then the enemy couldn't be too far away. "Stay inside, I'm going to go see if I can find out what's going on."

Grabbing her bonnet and shawl Jennie made her way out the door and down the steps. A few moments later she was standing on the corner of Baltimore and Breckinridge Streets with several other citizens, all of them hoping for news. Mr. Rupp was there, from the tannery down the street. Hatless, he hadn't even bothered to remove his stained leather apron. Maria was there as well, flour dusting her hands and apron. Knowing her better than anyone else on the street, Jennie moved in her direction. Mr. Rupp approached them both. "So, here we are once more on the fine streets of our fair town, watching soldiers march by and wondering what it all means and what it has in store for us. This is getting to be quite a common occurrence around here, wouldn't you say?"

Maria folded her arms in front of herself and shook her head.

Jennie adjusted the shawl around her shoulders and agreed with Mr. Rupp. "Too common, indeed. But what does it all mean now?"

"I'm not really sure, but as long as they are wearing the right color uniform I will not question it too much, if you understand my meaning."

"I do understand. But there are so many of them, so much more than when the Porter Guards were here a few winters ago. It must mean something more than a mere drill. Tel me they're not staying this time, that they're simply marching through to parts farther away."

"I wish I could, my dear, but I simply do not know what this latest invasion, friendly or not, means."

Looking around, Jennie could see townspeople leaning out of windows, cheering the soldiers as they marched north out of town towards the Chambersburg Pike. To her eye it looked as if the whole town had turned out into the street to watch the mounted soldiers go by. Those that weren't leaning out of windows or standing in their yards were sitting on the very roofs, yelling and cheering the soldiers on. The soldiers, in turn, were waving back, some of them even removing hats in recognition of their fine reception. The whole thing had a party atmosphere! Caught up in the moment, Jennie herself waved a hankie at the cavalry soldiers riding by. "What do you think Maria? Don't they look grand?"

"They do, indeed! A much better and more welcome sight than those nasty, dirty Rebel soldiers that were here not too long ago. The very sight of them, with their dirty, unkempt clothes and filthy bodies was enough to send a person screaming in the opposite direction. I do hope we have seen the last of them. But, tell me, where do you suppose all of these fine boys are heading?"

Mr. Rupp, who had left the women for a few minutes to talk to another neighbor passing by in a wagon, returned to share with them what he had heard. "Pardon me, ladies, but I have learned that these soldiers are under the command of General Buford and they are about setting up camp on the north end of town near the Lutheran Seminary. They are mostly a scouting party making sure those Rebel devils don't cross the Maryland border into our own Pennsylvania again."

"Is there a chance of that, do you think," asked Maria.

"Oh, I hardly doubt it. Did you see how many of these fine soldiers are marching through town? Why, there must be thousands of them! Surely that is enough to chase away whatever Rebel soldiers might be thinking of coming back this way."

"I pray you're right," added Jennie, pocketing her hankie and bringing her shawl back up around her shoulders. "The breeze is cooler now, and it looks like rain. I hope those boys of ours will be all right camping out in the rain tonight."

Maria gave her a quick hug, pulling her close and smiling. "I'm sure they will be just fine. Camping out in all kinds of weather is nothing new to them. Didn't Jack tell you that they have gum blankets to wrap up in to keep the dampness away?"

Jennie returned a sheepish grin, surprised that her private thoughts of Jack were found out. "Yes, he did mention that a time or two in his letters."

Mr. Rupp sensed a private conversation between the two women and moved on to talk to still another neighbor watching the parade of passing mounted soldiers.

"When was the last time you heard from him, dear?"

"Oh, it's been awhile now, I'm afraid, at least a few months."

"Which means nothing with this war going on, and you know it. Mailbags are constantly getting intercepted, misplaced and even lost! I'm sure he's just fine, probably sitting around a campfire this very minute penning you a letter full of '*I miss you Jennie's, how are you Jennie, why haven't you written Jennie?*'"

Jennie sensed the teasing quality in her friend's tone and quickly pulled away, laughing. "Oh, I know I'm being silly, but I simply cannot help it. It's one thing to read about the war in the paper or hear about it from the hawkers on the street, it's quite another to see it up close this way, with soldiers marching past our very doors. I see Jack in every blue uniform that passes by, and I can't help but wonder where he is, or what he's doing, and why I haven't heard from him."

The first few drops of rain began to lightly fall, causing the women to glance upwards, gauging the darkness of the clouds and wondering how much rain they might expect and how long it might fall. "Well, guess I better get back to Harry and Isaac."

"And I to my Henry. I have dinner done and warming on the stove, but heaven knows that man doesn't know how to get it from the pan onto a plate for consumption without my help."

Both women chuckled at the notion of such a helpless man and, waving good-bye, they went their separate ways.

Later that night, after the boys had been fed, prayers said, and tucked into bed, Jennie listened to the rain softly tapping on her bedroom window. She imagined that it was Jack tossing pebbles from the street below in an effort to get her attention. It always worked, just as it did now. With his picture propped up on the bedside table, she reached into her apron pocket for his latest letter. It was dated April, over two months old, but she reread it still one more time. The fold creases were getting more pronounced, making it harder to read the words written there, but it didn't matter. She had it all memorized anyway, and could recite it word for word even in the dark. The letter was getting heavy in her hands, as sleep took more hold. Jerking herself awake, she folded the letter carefully and replaced it in her apron pocket. Then, getting on her knees, she said her nightly prayers before crawling into bed, finally letting the rain lull her to sleep.

Chapter 9

Gettysburg

Wednesday, July 1, 1863

"Love your enemies, bless them that curse you,
do good to them that hate you,
and pray for them which despitefully use you and persecute
you."
Matthew 5:44

Jennie woke with the singing of the birds. The first rays of light were streaming in through the slightly open window, and peaking through the weaves of the lace curtain. Along with it came the sounds of a small town waking up. A horse galloping down Washington Street, a wagon being driven down Baltimore Street, and jays and crows yelling at the world.

It still seemed strange being alone in this house with just the boys, and she looked forward to the day when her mother would be back home where she belonged. The house took on more dimensions when she was alone in it she noticed, suddenly seeming larger than it truly was.

The sound of a woman screaming at a barking dog

brought her fully awake. Sitting up in bed she stretched her arms far above her head, letting out a wide yawn at the same time. Nature was calling, so she quietly made her way down the stairs to the necessary out back. Upon returning to the house she was thrilled to be greeted by silence. The boys were not yet awake. Good, she would be able to get her Bible reading in without disruption for a change. She knew, as she made her way back up the stairs that she would read it again, with them, after breakfast, but it was still enjoyable to read The Good Book quietly, by oneself. Turning to the book of Mathew, she read all of chapter five before the sounds of giggling brought her up short. The boys were finally awake.

"Hey! Be quiet in there," she admonished. The giggling stopped instantly, but only momentarily. Seconds later it started up again, quickly bursting into outright laughter.

Jennie softly closed The Bible. It was 5AM, and her day had officially begun.

Later, after breakfast and the boys Bible reading, she left them playing in the corner with wooden blocks and horses, while she went into the tailor shop to work. She had several small mending projects she wanted to finish before moving on to the new dress Mrs. Sullivan wanted her to make for her. The material was a lovely pumpkin color, with dark green vines and plum-colored flowers strewn through it. It was going to make a truly lovely gown, and she knew just the right trim that would set it off to perfection. She really couldn't wait to start on it, but first things first. Grabbing up a pair of trousers with no knees, Jennie searched through the scrap basket for a proper patch. It was still early morning, around eight o'clock, when a loud, unfamiliar sound brought her up short. The boys stopped their chattering and it seemed as if the house itself was holding its breath, wondering what was going on. Suddenly it came again, louder this time, shaking the very floorboards of the house.

"Jennie, what's going on?" It was Harry, calling from the other room.

"I don't know, but I'm about to go find out. You boys stay right here. Promise me you won't go out of the house."

"We promise." Both boys shook their heads earnestly, so Jennie grabbed a bonnet and dashed out the front door to see what was going on. She was half way down the steps before she remembered the parade of cavalry troops that came into town only yesterday. Her heart started beating faster, her feet rushing to keep up with her heart beat. The booming sounds they heard, and the vibrations all suddenly making sense.

Jennie looked ahead to the corner of Breckinridge Street and the Baltimore Pike and for once didn't see townspeople gathering, asking each other what was going on. No, this time they were screaming, running for cover and heading south, out of town. She just managed to grab the sleeve of young Tillie Pierce before she and the Schriver family she was with disappeared into the crowd with the rest of the panicked townspeople. "Tillie! Mrs. Schriver! Wait up!"

"Oh, Jennie, I can't! Haven't you heard? Can't you see? The Rebels have returned with a vengeance. They're streaming in from Chambersburg, and there's so many of them, Jennie! I don't think our boys can hold them back!"

"But where are you all going?"

"My family, the Weikert's, have a farm outside of town," answered Mrs. Schriver. She, her two little girls and Tillie all had small bundles tucked under their arms. Mrs. Schriver adjusted hers in order to grip her daughter's hand more firmly. "We should be safe there, I hope. And you should leave, too, if you know what's good for you. They say the Rebels are going to shell the whole town!"

As if to confirm what she just said, another explosion, louder than all of the rest, shook the very ground they were standing on, sending already panicked pedestrians screaming and running for cover.

"See what I mean? Hurry Jennie! Leave while there's still time!"

Another sound, more ominous than the booming cannon suddenly filled the air. Slowly Jennie realized it had been there all along, but so faint as to be unrecognizable. Now it was growing louder, getting closer. It was the sound of musket fire. Swallowing the lump in her throat, Jennie turned and ran back to the house as fast as she could. Up the steps she dashed, almost breaking down the door in her haste to get inside. The boys were still in the corner where she had left them, their eyes big as saucers as she hurried into the room. It took all of her willpower to pretend a calm she didn't feel in order not to frighten the boys any more than they already were.

"Harry, I need you to do me a big favor."

"What, Jennie?" She noted the quiver in his voice, but his back was straight, his shoulders squared, like Jack had taught him to do before he left town. He was the epitome of the perfect little soldier, and she loved him all the more for it.

"Go grab the big carpet bag and fill it with extra clothes for you and Issac. We're going to go and stay with Mama and Georgia until this is all over. While you're doing that I'm going to carry Isaac over to the house. I'll come back for you directly and for whatever else they might need over there. They're bound to need more food with all of the extra mouths to feed, and maybe some quilts and blankets, too. Now, you are not to leave this house for any reason until I return. Do you understand?"

"Yes, Jennie, clothes and food and don't go outside."

"That's right. You're such a brave young man, Harry. Now, come, Isaac, we must hurry so that I can come back and h e l p   H a r r y . "

"Jennie, wait! How long are you gonna be gone?"

"I don't know, Harry, but I'll go as fast as I can. Just stay inside and gather up some extra blankets and clothes. You'll be all right." Jennie disappeared out the door with Isaac in her arms, and Harry hurried with his chore.

Mary Wade didn't look surprised when Jennie showed

up at the door, Isaac in hand. "My child, you look all worn out! Where's Harry, is everything all right?" Between gulps of air she struggled to tell her mother everything she had heard and witnessed, but Mary Wade had already heard the same stories from the people passing by on their way out of town. The two women shared a brief hug, and moments later Jennie was hurrying the few blocks back to Breckenridge Street for her brother and whatever else she could carry.

Harry was staring out the upstairs bedroom window when Jennie entered. A bundle of clothes tied in a blanket lay on the bed, proof that he had been busy in her absence. The look of relief on his face upon seeing her was clearly evident and brought a quick smile to Jennie's lips. "Has it been that bad," she asked, grabbing another carpetbag and tucking her own things tucked inside - clothes, hairbrush, and her Bible.

Harry straightened up, adding several inches to his height. "Not really, just some more explosions. But I think they're getting closer."

Jennie resisted the urge to tussle his hair. He was trying so hard to be the brave young man of the house. Jack's picture stood on the dresser and she hurried across the room to snatch it up. For a moment she stared into his face. Funny, she thought, he looks different somehow. Maybe it was the sounds of battle raging outside or her heightened state of fear, but his eyes seemed to have lost that all powerful liveliness, that uncanny ability to follow her every motion through the room.

"Jennie, are you almost ready to go?" Harry broke her silent reverie.

Quickly Jennie slipped Jack's picture into her apron pocket, along with the last letter he had sent. A few minutes later she had gathered up the extra foodstuffs, tying them up in a large kitchen towel.

The booming from the north end of town seemed not to want to stop. But already the screams of the townspeople had died down. Those that were staying behind had already found a safe place to weather out the storm, and those that want to leave were on the roads heading south out of town. Jennie hustled Harry out the door and turned to lock it behind them. Dropping the key into her apron pocket she gave the door one last jerk, testing the lock. It held, but for the first time she realized what a lose-fitting door they had lived behind all these years. And up until now it had always seemed enough. But now, with enemy soldiers about to descend upon the town, she wondered if their simple door, locked or unlocked, would be enough to keep anyone away, let alone angry, determined soldiers.

"Jennie! Hurry up!" Harry was halfway to the corner, his pack slung over his back while he impatiently waited for his sister to catch up.

Without another thought, Jennie patted her apron pocket, felt the weight of the key and Jack's picture and letter, and hurried down the steps to her brother. She was actually amazed to still see so many people on the streets. Granted there were not as many as earlier in the morning, but there were still small groups of whole families grabbing what they could carry and hurrying away from danger. One thing she did notice were the many free black families rushing out of town. They were probably carrying the least of all, and there couldn't possibly be any left in town. As the sounds of battle increased to the north of them, she couldn't help but feel sorry for those poor black families who, more than anyone else, were running for their very lives. She had heard the stories of blacks captured by southern soldiers being sent back into the deep south as slaves, even if they were born free. Adjusting the bundle on her back she tried to hustle Harry along faster, the threat of enemy soldiers prepared to ransack her home a scary enough threat for her.

By the time they made it to Georgia's house the two were out of breath. Isaac seemed glad and relieved to see Harry again, and the two huddled in a corner of the front parlor, out of everyone's way. Georgia was sitting up in bed, nursing tiny Louis, while their mother stood in the kitchen, getting a pot of water ready for tea. "Is it bad out there, dear?"

"As bad as it can get, Mama. The streets are getting pretty quiet now, as far as townspeople go, but the sounds of that battle seem to be getting louder every time I stick my head out the door."

Mrs. Wade wiped her hands on her apron, a gesture of dismissing the subject as much as to dry her hands. "So, what did you bring us from the house? I hope you pretty much cleaned out the cupboards. No point in leaving anything behind for those thieving Rebels."

"Mother, please, they're not all 'thieving Rebels.' Remember, Wesley is counted in their number."

"So, he is. And when was the last time you laid eyes on him, hmm? You don't know how much he might have changed, or what kind of young man he has grown into. War changes a person, why he might not be any different than any of those other dirty, unkempt, miserable looking southern boys we've been seeing of late. They look quite capable of doing just about anything to put some food in their belly or shoes on their feet."

"And if that's true, would you begrudge them that morsel of food Mama?"

"No, of course not dear."

"Well, that's all I'm saying. And besides, I talked to Wesley's sister Julia just the other day, and even though she hasn't heard from him in a long time she insists he's still reading his Bible on a daily basis, which has to say something about his character, wouldn't you say?"

"You know what, young lady, I'm sorry I brought it up in the first place. Hand me that tin of tea, the water is ready now, and let's not bring this subject up again."

Jennie helped pour the tea and get a light snack of biscuits and jam for everyone in the household. The sugar, flour, salt and other foodstuffs she had brought from home were added to what Georgia already had in her own cupboards. The extra blankets were set aside, and the two carpetbags of clothes were

172

hauled upstairs into the bedroom to alleviate clutter downstairs. It seemed they had barely gotten settled in when increased activity in the street captured their attention. Jennie and Mrs. Wade, still in the kitchen, paused over the dishes they were washing and glanced towards the parlor room door. Harry's footsteps could be heard running across the wood floor to the front window, and tiny Louis wailed as Georgia sat up for a closer look.

"Harry, child, what's going on," Mrs. Wade asked as she made her way into the living room. The sounds of battle seemed right in front of the house now, and they could distinctly hear men shouting, screaming sometimes in pain. Her hand flew to her throat at the sight of so many soldiers in blue in the street and yard in front of the house. "Oh, My Lord in Heaven," she cried, pulling Harry away from the window and closing the curtain tightly.

"Mama, please, what is it?" Georgia was frantically trying to shush her screaming infant, all the while staring at her mother, hoping for an answer to her question.

Just then they heard the sound of the back door opening. Jennie had stepped from the kitchen onto the backyard stoop, the need for a better look and answers spurring her on. What she saw had her rooted to the spot. The horrible sight of their own men in blue running in panic towards the outskirts of town, just like the townspeople before them. She felt sick, was as if something physical was drawing the very breath from her lungs. They were in a rout! The Union army was leaving town, abandoning them to the will of the enemy soldiers! Could it get any worse?

She had no idea how long she stood there, hand to her throat, watching the number of fleeing soldiers increase, with no one trying to stop the tide. Even the officers were running away, determination on all of their faces. At some point Jennie became aware of Louis crying, and shouts from inside the house, all directed towards her.

"Jennie get in here immediately!"

"Jennie, what are you thinking?"

"What are you doing?"

"Get in here and shut that door!"

But Jennie did none of that. A soldier, one of the boys in blue, fell in the front yard only feet away from where she stood. He wasn't hurt, at least no wound that Jennie could perceive. But he looked at her with pleading eyes, begging for a drink of water. And Jennie didn't hesitate. Running down the few steps, she hurried to the well and filled the bucket. With cup in hand she lifted the soldiers head, comforting him, and allowing him to drink his fill. All too soon she found herself surrounded by others, all demanding the same cool refreshment. The first man vanished in the crowd as Jennie filled up the water bucket time and again. Finally taking a stance near the street, she handed cup after cup of water to the passing soldiers, picking up pieces of information as they passed. And the information was not good.

"The rebels had taken the field!"

"The rebels had taken the town!"

"Thousands were being made prisoner!"

"The battle was lost."

"Save yourself!"

She heard one mumble something about Fredericksburg as he stumbled past, but she didn't know what he meant, and he was gone before she could ask. She thought, at first, that he had merely confused Gettysburg with Fredericksburg. But when he said it again with such grief and despair in his voice, she wondered if he was perhaps thinking of home. She knew how she would feel if she were far away from home, lost, without friends and family members, and enemy bullets seeking her out at every turn. Hastily she scooped up another draught of water for still another soldier in blue, concentrating on the faces before her now, and not those of Jack, John, Louis or Wesley.

Still, for every naysayer that came her way, there was another soldier full of spirit who told her not to lose heart. They would regroup and still chase those horrid traitors from this soil! The Rebels would not live to ravish another inch of their homeland!

And so Jennie waited, as did they all. Standing by the side of the dirt road, drenched from the waist down, she dolled out water with her cup, or filled canteens for those that had them. No one walked away without Jennie wishing, 'God's blessings' upon them.

The day was hot, made more so by anxiety, fear, and the physical exertion of battle. All day the men streamed by, dirty, sweaty, tired, hungry and thirsty. While Jennie stood in the sun, aiding those with a thirst, her mother was in the kitchen, preparing bread and biscuits for the hungry. Some, motivated by fear of death or capture didn't even bother to stop on their race southward. She wondered how far south they might run before realizing that wasn't such a good idea either.

Around supper time the Union soldiers panicked rout through town slowly came to an crawl. But then a new horror began. Sharpshooters from both sides began shooting at each other, and Georgia's house seemed to be caught right in the middle of the crossfire. Not for the first time did Jennie wonder if there was any safe place in or near this town today.

Inside, the house seemed only slightly less chaotic. Georgia leaned over the bed, changing a very red-faced, disagreeable baby whose fists were clenched in rage and whose lungs were getting more than their fair share of exercise. Harry was demonstrating to a squealing Isaac a new way of getting him around the house, by dragging him across the floor on a blanket, sled fashion. Mary Wade was in the kitchen noisily tossing wood into the stove in dinner preparations, and over all the din, minnie balls and bullets wizzed by the house, sometimes striking the bricks outside and making a loud whine.

As Jennie closed the back door, Mary Wade glanced up at her daughter. "Look at you. I haven't seen that much mud on one garment since Harry tried wading across Rock Creek, missed, and fell in." Her eyes, once more busy on the task of cutting up carrots in bite size pieces, held no reproach, and her voice held no condemnation. "Go on with you, get upstairs and out of that dress before you catch your death."

Jennie held out her skirt, inspecting it for the first time. "It'll dry fast enough in this heat, I imagine. Would you like me to start on the potatoes?"

"Well if you care to. But really, dear, you look all in. I can manage this if you care to change and rest for a few minutes."

"No, Mama, I'll be fine. Hand me that knife, won't you?"

In no time the two women had stew on the stove and bread in the oven. Though they never got used to the sounds of fighting, they learned not to flinch every time a minnie ball went sailing past the house or ricocheted off the wall. At least they weren't penetrating and coming inside, which made them feel relatively safe.

Dinnertime came and Georgia joined them all at the kitchen table. Little Louis was asleep on the bed, and gathering together in the kitchen for a meal seemed like such a normal thing to do under very extraordinary circumstances. Together they said the common table prayer, and as the sun went down they served up portions of thin beef stew and bread warm from the oven.

But the calm of the evening meal could not shut out the sounds of the battle weary world outside. Frenzied shouting, rushing horses, cries from the wounded, and the ever persistent sound of minnie balls sought them out, forcing them to pay attention. "I can't bear the thought of my Louis being in such a battle. Where is he right now, I wonder? I do hope he's safe," Georgia pleaded.

"And our John," added Mary Wade.

"Yes, John, and Jennie's Jack, too," agreed Georgia, reaching for her sister's hand. Even as they clasped hands in support, Jennie felt Jack's picture and endearing note burning into her flesh. Tears welled in her eyes, until she jumped to her feet and angrily wiped them away. "I will not fret over what I cannot control. God is watching over them. But if I must listen to that poor soldier moaning in the yard one more minute I will surely go crazy!" Grabbing a cup of water and a clean rag from the box by the door, she ran out the back door into the waning light.

*　　　*　　　*　　　*

*

"Get a move on there! On the double quick! Let's go! Let's go! Let's go!"

Wesley Culp hurried along with the rest of his unit. Darkness was coming on fast, and there was no doubt in his mind now that they were heading straight for the town of his birth – Gettysburg. The road they traveled was familiar, the houses and barns they passed were familiar, the trees, the lay of the land, even the very stones beneath his bare feet were all familiar. Well, maybe not the very stones, he argued with himself, but everything else was pure home. The sudden realization that he was this close once more filled him with mixed emotions. He had dreamed of coming home again some day, especially of late, but not this way. Not wearing this grey uniform and carrying a loaded musket intent on mischief. No, his recent thoughts of home centered more on Annie and Julia, warm embraces and smiles, home-cooked meals eaten with utensils on real plates while sitting on chairs at a table, a real bed

177

with clean sheets and blankets, maybe a nice hot bath and a shave. Those are the thoughts he had of home, not this skulking through the near dark on the back roads into town.

"Hurry up, I say! Old Alleghany Johnson is waiting for you boys over by yonder hill! Now move it!"

It was so odd having to follow a new commander into the field. Things were different when Stonewall was around. Actually, Wesley reflected, things were much harder when Stonewall was around. That man would march your legs off up to the kneecap and not think twice about it. Ah, how he missed that man! Marching and fighting seemed so much different then, like there was a special purpose to all of it. Now it was getting old, more like drudgery than an idea filled with principle. It was as if the very spark had gone out of the war, and all a person wanted was to see the war come to a close, whichever way it went. *Just end it already!*

"You men! Right here! Form up right here and hunker down! Wait for further orders!"

Wesley and the others almost laughed at that one – *Wait for further orders*! As if any of them had done anything on their own since signing their name or marking their mark when they joined up. It occurred to him that he might not be able to live on his own, outside the army, without someone around telling him when to wake up, when to sleep, when to eat, and when to head to the latrine. But he would certainly like to give it a try!

The men had sat down, some of them going immediately to sleep. Wesley crossed his legs, laid his musket across his lap and used it as a brace for his elbows. Crickets and frogs filled the evening air with song, as if cheering on the coming night. Wesley welcoming it, too, welcomed the opportunity to breathe in this air filled with scents and thoughts of home. But along with the eagerness to see his family and home once more came the trepidation of what it might cost him. He was a soldier, a soldier that had signed on to kill Yankees. But he knew that a battle that was fought anywhere near a town increased the likelihood that civilians might be injured or worse still, killed. He had seen with his own eyes what happens to homes, barns, churches, stores and other buildings when a battle gets too close. Suddenly he hoped that their being here was only momentary, that they would regroup here, go around Gettysburg and simply move on. He would gladly forfeit the chance to see Annie and Julia once more if it meant keeping them safe. His hands were still folded in prayer when Ben and Ned approached.

"Say, Wes, they say that town up ahead there is Gettysburg, Pennsylvania. Isn't that where you hail from?"

"Uh huh."

"Well, ain't you glad to be so close to home?"

"I'm not sure." Wesley looked from one friend to the next before turning his attention towards Gettysburg, the rooftops of some of the buildings the only thing visible from their vantage point.

"Pardon me for saying this, friend, but you don't look so excited to be this close to home, lease wise not as far as I can tell." Ben lost interest in the roof tops of Gettysburg, turning his attention instead to a large grasshopper that decided the barrel of his musket looked like as good a place as any to take a rest.

"Deep down, I guess I'm not all that excited."

"Well, why not, for goodness sake?"

"Did you see what we did to Fredericksburg, Chambersburg, and Winchester?"

"Well, to be fair, that twern't just us, ya know."

"Doesn't matter, Ned. This is my home town, I don't want anything like that to happen here. I would feel personably responsible for everything that goes wrong, you understand?"

"Yeah, I guess, when you put it that way. But are you at least gonna try and get into town and see your kin?"

"I hadn't quite thought that far ahead. Maybe, if we stick around here long enough."

"Oh, we're going to be here awhile, I reckon. I hear tell that Longstreet and his corps is over there." Ned pointed vaguely towards the north. A. P. Hill is over there, too, and even Marse Robert hisself is around here someplace. All we need is that pretty boy cavalry leader, General Stuart, and we will be a force to reckon with, that's for sure."

Ben shook his head with the wonder of it all. "Wouldn't surprise me none if we marched right over and through that town tomorrow."

Ned punched him in the arm, hard.

"Hey! What was that for?" Ben glared at his friend, rubbing his arm in pain.

"For being such an idiot, that's what for!"

Wesley had had enough of his friends' well-meaning conversation. Rising to his feet he wandered off in search of a place to gaze at more than just rooftops of his boyhood town. But it was already getting dark, and some of the boys were gathering wood to make fires and cook their dinner. No further orders had come down, so it looked as if they would at least be spending the night here. Wesley glanced over at the large farmhouse off to his left. Nestled at the base of a hill, he had withheld that bit of information from his friends. The fact that the hill was named for his family, Culp's Hill, and that house belonged to his Uncle Henry. From where he sat it looked as if no one was home, but the darkened house could very well be misleading. There was still a modicum of daylight left, and Uncle Henry was always very frugal when it came to wasting candles. His adage was to go to bed with the sun and rise with it because that's what The Lord intended. Wesley smiled at the remembrance of Uncle Henry reciting those words almost every time they'd sit down to dinner together. It drove the women in the family crazy because they wouldn't be done talking yet and Uncle Henry would make a show of going upstairs to bed. He almost laughed out loud when he remembered how quickly the women would move to say their good-byes before calling it a night themselves. More memories, large and small, drifted through Wesley's mind like fluff from a cottonwood tree. Some of them, more poignant than others, lingered in his head, taunting him with their realism, like some harlot on a street corner before another one came along to take its place. Almost before he knew it, he had made up his mind to get into town somehow and see his sister's, Annie and Julia. The one thought that plagued him most was the reaction of those he had known back then to his wearing of the grey now. As irksome as it would be, he was sure they wouldn't listen to any explanation on his part, and to their credit, he was just as sure that he wouldn't be able to explain it himself. Because the truth was, it quite literally – just happened. He got wrapped up in the moment. And who knew the war was going to last this long anyway? Yes, that would sound real good and make a lot of sense to someone who just had their house blown down around their ears. He sighed, shook his head and glanced up at the heavens. The stars were brilliant tonight, brighter than he remembered seeing them – ever! Perhaps it was their way of welcoming him home. Wesley took this as a good sign, and knew that his sisters, at least, would welcome him with open arms.

Chapter 10

Gettysburg

Thursday, July 2, 1863

"Have not I commanded thee?
Be strong and of good courage; be not afraid,
neither be thou dismayed:
for the Lord they God is with thee withersoever thou goest."
Joshua 1:9

No one slept in the tiny house on the Baltimore Pike that night. Though the sounds of battle had abated during the nighttime hours, other sounds, unusual and disturbing, continued throughout the darkest hours. The sounds of cavalry horses going down the street, soldiers running around the house, digging trenches, gosh knows where, hopefully not in the garden, were non-stop. But it was the pitiful cries of the wounded, laying somewhere, out there, out of sight, but not far enough away from the window to be undetected that caused everyone the most distress. There were so many of them, and the doctors were so few. Jenny and her mother did what she could before sheer exhaustion forced her to seek solace inside the house, if only for awhile.

All of the windows in the house were open, the better for any stray breeze to enter. The upstairs bedroom was stifling, forcing everyone to gather in the downstairs front parlor. Too, the very thought of separating, with some going upstairs to sleep, was such an unwelcome notion, that all quickly dismissed the idea.

Georgia and the baby had the bed, but there was room for Mrs. Wade to lay down as well. Jennie grabbed what sleep she could curled up on the sofa beneath the window. Too exhausted to change, Jennie and her mother slept fully clothed.

Before the first weak rays of sunshine could seek out the corners of their room, the awful sounds of cannon shot, flying bullets, whining minnie balls, and the screams and shouts of soldiers filled the air once more. All of them woke with a start.

A very weary Jennie opened her eyes, immediately meeting those of her mother. "Good morning," mother greeted daughter in a voice hoarse with sleep.

Jennie struggled to her feet, resisting the urge to stretch luxuriously. "This is the day which the Lord hath made," she said, rubbing sleep from her eyes.

A minnie ball chose that moment to ricochet off the corner of the house. Shocked, but not unduly frightened, both women quickly glanced up. "We will be glad and rejoice in it," Mrs. Wade added.

Motioning to the kitchen, she bade Jennie follow. "Looks like there'll be no more sleeping around here today, we might as well get at it. I'm sure our boys out there are working up a powerful hunger with all that fighting. They'll be wanting their biscuits soon."

Moments later, the small house was alive with cautious activity. Georgia saw to changing and cleaning her infant son. Harry and Isaac moved their mattress beneath the bed in an attempt to be out of harms way, both from the wayward bullet and the misplaced foot. Jennie helped her mother in the kitchen, thankful that a kind soldier had brought them a load of kindling wood for their fire the night before. Though he insisted the act didn't require payment, it was clear that a few biscuits wouldn't be refused either.

The women worked silently, each absorbed in their own

thoughts and chores. Ingredients were measured, mixed and stirred, and when dough was left to rise, they moved on to other chores.

A large blast, close to the house, shook it so hard the women felt it would shake right off its foundation. Georgia and the boys let out a scream, and Jennie had to cover her mouth to keep from screaming herself. Mrs. Wade stopped in her kneading of bread dough, her face ashen. But when she realized that the house was still standing over them and that no one was hurt, she quickly turned back to the task at hand.

Jennie let out a quick, hysterical burst of laughter. "Did you ever think you could get used to such sounds, Mama?"

"Who said I was used to it?"

Mother and daughter shared a quick, though tremulous smile, wiped their brows with their aprons and got quickly back to work.

They had barely finished their baking preparations when the first knock sounded at the door. Jennie, the closest, answered the summons. As expected, a blue-clad soldier stood on the step, hat in hand. The smile he flashed her was genuine, if apologetic. "Mornin', miss. I was jest wonderin..."

But Jennie knew what he wanted before the words left his mouth, knew before she even answered the door. "I'm sorry, soldier, they're aren't quite ready yet. If you could come back in half an hour, we might have some fresh biscuits for you then."

"Yes, ma'am. Thank you, ma'am. I surely will be back, ma'am." The soldier was repositioning the cap on his head when Mrs. Wade spoke up from the kitchen. "Don't bring too many of your friends with you when you come. It appears we only have enough flour for one more batch of biscuits and two loaves of bread. That isn't going to go too far the way you boys like to eat."

The soldier, an older man with greying hair, heard Mrs. Wade clearly. Removing his hat once more, he stepped closer to the door and ventured a proposition. "If I was to come up with some more flour, would you be willing to make us some more bread?"

Jennie stepped aside while her mother seemed to take over the conversation. Wiping her hands on her apron, her mother approached the two of them standing at the door. "Well, soldier, from what I understand the rebels are in full control of this town. They're out there right now, firing on this house day and night, and shooting anyone who dares show their nose on Baltimore Street. Further more, every store and market has either hidden their goods, sent them out of town for safe keeping, or had them confiscated by the rebel soldiers. Just how do you propose to find us any flour at all?"

But the Union soldier seemed completely unconcerned by the bleak picture Mrs. Wade painted. "All I need to know, ma'am, is are you willing to make us the bread? You just leave getting the flour up to me."

Mrs. Wade hesitated only a moment, pondering the incongruity of standing in the kitchen of her daughter's house carrying on an everyday business conversation while a battle raged all around. Wrapping an affectionate arm around Jennie's waist, she nodded her head. "Bring us the flour soldier, and we'll see you get all the bread and biscuits we can bake up."

Within an hour the soldier was back, a hefty fifty-pound sack of flour slung over his shoulder. He deposited it in a corner of the kitchen, winked at Jennie, tipped his hat in salute to her mother, and walked out whistling a merry tune.

The minute the door closed behind him, Mrs. Wade rushed to Jennie's side, whispering conspiratorially. "Your sister's birthday is the day after tomorrow. With everything in such short supply, we may never get another chance to bake her a little cake. How wrong do you suppose it would be to save a portion of this flour to bake her something special?"

Jennie glanced over her shoulder, making sure Georgia wasn't within earshot. "I was thinking the same thing, Mama. I suppose if we make it a big enough cake to share with the soldier who made such a thing possible, no one would rightly complain."

"Very well, then. I'll set some aside, and tomorrow we'll make her a cake she won't soon forget."

"And maybe tomorrow the rebels will be gone, and I can run back home to get the hankies I made her for her birthday. I tatted the edges of two of them for her myself."

"How wonderfully thoughtful. I know she'll love them. I made her something, too; some lavender sachet's, her favorite scent."

Engaging in simple, happy, trivial conversations, life within the small, brick home soon took on a sense of routine. Georgia, for the most part, stayed in the front room, caring for her baby and trying to keep young Harry and Isaac calm. It proved to be an unending job, as she screamed with each bullet or minnie ball that struck the house, thereby causing the boys to scream as well. After scrambling out from under the bed several times, they decided to just stay put, covering their ears, and watching Georgia's feet as she paced back and forth with the irritable infant.

In the kitchen, Jennie and her mother continued their unremitting chore of baking bread and biscuits. The constantly fired oven made the room quite unbearable. Several times Jennie was tempted to open the back door for ventilation, but the threat of flying missiles of any kind kept her from following through. Soon, both women had rivulets of perspiration running down their necks, coating their faces in a perpetual sheen.

While the bread was in the oven the household took a momentary rest. Jennie picked up her Bible, sharing her daily devotion aloud with them all. Opening The Book to Genesis, chapter seventeen, she began reading the story of Isaac, because she knew her young charge enjoyed it so. The others in the room couldn't help smile at the way his face lit up when he heard his name mentioned in the huge book resting in Jennie's lap. "And God said, Sarah they wife shall bear thee a son indeed; and thou shalt call his name Isaac: and I will establish my covenant with him for an everlasting covenant, and with his seed after him." If only temporarily, the few people in the tiny home were able to shut out the sounds of battle, ignore their own physical discomfort and fear, and concentrate on adventures that took place long ago.

"What's that smell?" Harry was pinching his nostrils and making an awful face.

Isaac immediately followed suit. "Yeah, something stinks!"

"The bread! Oh, my, goodness, we're burning the bread!" Both Mrs. Wade and Jennie flew to their feet and made a dash for the kitchen. The oven door was flung open, and Mrs. Wade used her apron to quickly retrieve the first of several loaves that had been set to bake. "Oh, dear, oh, dear," she continued to mutter.

"Don't worry, Mama, they don't look that bad. They really don't," Jennie offered by way of consolation. "I doubt those hungry soldiers will even notice."

"But I'll notice! I wanted everything to be perfect for those poor, hungry men, and now just look at this!"

Jennie helped remove the rest of the loaves and set them on the table to cool. The crusts were a darker brown than usual, but she could hardly call them burned. Several more bullets hit the north side of the house on the upper level. Harry and Isaac scurried back under the bed and Georgia, standing in the doorway to the front parlor, hugged her baby closer to her breast. The close confines of the house, the lack of rest, and the constantly raging battle outside was beginning to take its toll on everyone.

Several minutes later, after calm had been restored, the bread was removed from their pans, cut into slices, and set aside for the first soldiers who would soon come knocking on the door. Though how they braved the hailstorm of bullets was anyone's guess.

Lunch time came and went, and still Jennie and her mother stopped only for the brief minute it took to swallow a few bites of canned peaches spread over their own fresh bread. Georgia made sure the boys came out from hiding long enough to eat their meal, allowing her mother and sister to continue their baking. Throughout the morning the bread and biscuits barely had time to cool completely before being swallowed up by the many Union soldiers that came knocking at their door. Jennie never learned whether it was word of mouth or a fragrant breeze that brought the soldiers unerringly to their door, and it didn't really matter. The fact was, she was doing what little she could to help those so far from home and in so much need.

All morning and into the afternoon Jennie and her mother worked in the overheated kitchen. Perspiration soaked their dresses, while exhaustion seeped into their tired limbs. During lulls in the fighting, Jennie would go outside to aid the boys in blue by filling canteens, and bringing cups of water to the wounded ones working their way behind the Union line on Cemetery Hill. The home became a sort of beacon, the aroma of baking bread and the site of a young woman dolling out water more than the haggard soldiers could refuse. In spite of the heat of the day, the kitchen was still hotter, and the fresh air and hurried conversations with the soldiers filled Jennie with a sense of purpose that toiling alone could not. Every soldier that sipped from her cup was Jack, every one that told her get back inside where it was safe was Jack, every one that stumbled, fell and had to be helped up was Jack. Back and forth to the well she ran, heedless of the water soaking her skirt and muddying her hem. They were all Jack, and they all needed her, needed her to be strong, needed her to...

A sound like roaring cannon split the air, the projectile landing somewhere in the street behind her. Most of the soldiers walked on, oblivious to the war raging all around them. Their steps were heavy, matching their countenance. Their eyes said they had seen enough horror to last a lifetime, and if God

Almighty wanted to take them home this very minute, that was all right with them. But there were others who were so close that the concussion knocked them right off their feet. One soldier, close by, dove at her, shielding her with his body. "You'd best get on inside, miss. 'pears things are gonna be heating up around here again," he said, helping her to her feet.

She hesitated, the shock of it all, and the violent, physical aspect of war so very foreign to her. The soldier, old enough to be her father, gave her a gentle shove towards the house. "Go on now. Git!" Shaken to the core, Jennie finally obeyed.

From the back door, her mother watched her walk the short distance to the house. It seemed to her that Jennie's steps matched those of the soldiers who had seen unimaginable horrors. The very air they breathed was alive with dust, dirt, smoke, and the ghastly sounds that had become so much a part of their life lately. She waited for her daughter, holding the back door open wide. Softly she closed the door behind them, an incongruous action given the noise of battle going on outside. And with the closing of the door the last of the cooling breeze left the small kitchen. Slowly the heat and sweet aroma of the kitchen enveloped them both once again. Knowing that her daughter wouldn't sit down to rest, as resting was impossible under the circumstances, she slid the dough tray across the table in her direction, while she busied herself measuring out flour for still another batch of biscuits. Before long the horror of the near miss was forgotten and busy hands once more filled the minutes and hours of another long day.

Later in the afternoon there was a lull in the sound of hungry soldiers knocking on their door, replaced instead by the increased hammering of bullets and minnie balls chinking away at the bricks of their sanctuary. Georgia had just left the kitchen, where she tried again to see if there was anything she could do to aid Jennie and her mother. Louis was sleeping at the foot of the bed, and Harry and Isaac were under it, curled up in the nest they had made for themselves. Suddenly the very ground beneath their feet trembled and shook as if a mighty earthquake had violated the town, or at least their small portion of it. A crash, louder than anything they had ever heard rocked the house above their heads. Instantly bricks and wood tumbled onto the floor upstairs, and plaster rained down from the ceiling. Every soul in the house screamed in panic. It was the final attack on Jennie's overwrought senses. She fainted to the floor, as the plaster dust from the ceiling liberally coated her and everyone else with its fine flour-like substance.

Georgia pushed herself up from the bed, seemingly surprised that she was still alive. Her eyes landed on Louis, but the baby hadn't awakened or even moved. Tears filled her eyes then, and slowly the sounds of the explosion were replaced by whimpering. Immediately she fell to her knees, searching under the bed for Harry and Isaac.

Mrs. Wade ran around the kitchen table to kneel by Jennie's side. Cradling her head in her lap, Mrs. Wade gently slapped her daughter's cheeks, hoping for a response. "Jennie! Jennie! Wake up! Are you all right?"

Finally, after a few moments, Jennie opened her eyes and began to mumble. "What happened?"

Mrs. Wade was just about to explain that she wasn't sure when Georgia came running down the stairs and into the kitchen. "Lord Almighty! You won't believe it, but a bomb went through the house and knocked a hole from our bedroom straight through to the McClain side of the house. I couldn't see where it landed, but I'm pretty sure it didn't go off, Praise God!"

"You mean it's up there still?"

"Yes, I'm quite certain it is, but there is so much debris in the way I can't make much of it. Still, it makes sense that if it had gone off or went through the house on the other side there would be a much bigger hole, don't you think?"

Mrs. Wade helped Jennie to her feet. "Yes, I'm sure you're right, dear."

A sudden pounding on the door behind them brought them all up short. Jennie whirled around, barely managing to squash the scream building up inside. A soldier's friendly voice greeted them from the other side. "Is everyone all right in there?"

Coming to her senses, Jennie opened the door. "Yes, we are all just fine, thank you."

The soldier stood there a moment, glanced in at the three women, and quickly removed his hat. His face and hands were black with soot and his uniform was so coated with dust that, at first glance, he could have been taken for a Rebel soldier in grey. It was impossible to tell how old he was. Bullets continued to ping the house periodically, and still the soldier stood there starring inside. "That's good," he finally said, and Jennie nodded. He seemed about to go, but then changed his mind and turned back around. "Pardon me for asking this, but you wouldn't happen to have any of that fine bread ready, would you?"

Under better circumstances Jennie might have laughed out loud, but the recent threat to the very roof over their heads followed so quickly by something so mundane as a piece of bread had her all off balance. Without hesitation she turned to her mother standing by the kitchen table. "Mama, will you hand me that plate of biscuits, please?"

Mrs. Wade, as dumfounded as her daughter, obediently handed her the plate of biscuits, now coated with plaster dust as well as flour. Still in shock, it didn't occur to her to apologize or explain their condition. She merely looked at them with uncomprehending eyes as the soldier stuffed several in his pockets and walked away with one in each hand. "Thank you kindly, ma'am. God bless you all!"

The soldier calmly walked away from the door, bullets were zinging by left and right, but he paid them no more mind than he would have if they had been snowflakes.

The simple routine act of passing out bread woke the

women from the shock that had settled over the household since the missile had stuck the house. Jennie closed the back door and almost cried with relief. "Oh, my, that poor man. I'm afraid he thinks that plaster dust was flour!"

"I believe you're right," agreed Mrs. Wade, reaching for a broom to start cleaning up.

"Should I go and stop him?"

"Don't you dare open that door, young lady! Besides, he's long gone by now and has probably devoured half of them already. Grab a rag and help me clean up this mess. We still have more work to do."

Georgia looked in on the boys, saw that they were both safely back under the bed and that the baby was still sound asleep. Grabbing a rag, she joined her sister and mother in the kitchen and helped to bring it back to its normally clean standard. Time was all but forgotten as they went through the repeated motions of measuring ingredients, mixing dough, stoking the fire, and making bread in the stifling hot kitchen. But it was no cooler in the front parlor where the drapes were all closed against the bright sun, and the windows were closed against, what, bullets? Several times they thought how silly an action that was, but no one dared stand in front of it to open it, preferring instead to deal with the heat. But there were those few moments when the back door was opened to pass out bread and biscuits to famished soldiers that Jennie was able to grab a breath of fresh air and get a look at the sky. Lower to the ground there was nothing but dust and smoke from the guns, but straight up, through the treetops, there was blue sky visible, with only the occasional passing white cloud to give dimension to that wide expanse. The white clouds, what few there were, rushed by as if they, too, were afraid to behold what was going on just below them. Locked up all day in the hot house, the cooling blue of the sky was a most beautiful sight, welcoming in its simplicity. But she also knew that it was a lie, that it wasn't as calm and simple as it looked. That in order to reach that serene, peaceful setting she would have to pass through the battle that raged all around them. Through the bullets that tore through flesh, heedlessly taking life with them as they went, or missiles that ripped into rooftops that sheltered sleeping babies. Down here was nothing but pain and calamity, the likes of which she never knew existed until recently. It was the stuff of novels and newspaper articles, all those sordid things that happened to people in far off places, not in tiny, tranquil Gettysburg where nothing but the mundane ever occurred.

The blue sky was forgotten as Jennie suddenly became aware of the soldier in front of her. He took a step closer, blocking out her view of that peaceful scene. His dirty hand was out in front of him, a few silver coins cupped in the palm. "Here you go, ma'am. I thank you kindly for the biscuits. They were the best I ever ate."

Shocked back to reality, Jennie was aware of the empty plate in her hand. A smile turned up the corner of her lips, a smile that was more outward appearance than anything she felt inside, where it really counted. "Oh, no, private, you keep that for yourself. I'm sure you'll find a better use for that somewhere down the road."

"Well, thank you kindly, ma'am. I know I speak for the rest of the boys when I say that the bread and biscuits coming from this here house is truly the best we've eaten in; well, I don't rightly remember when, and that's the truth of it. And trust me when I say that we'll do our best to keep you and everyone in this house safe."

"We certainly appreciate that." Jennie's smile brightened, lighting up her whole face this time. The private returned the smile, tipped his hat, and walked away around the corner of the house. A soft moan caught her attention just before she closed the door. Most of the shooting had stopped, however temporarily, and Jennie dared to step outside and see who was in need. Following the whimpering sounds, she found a wounded soldier propped up against a fence rail towards the back of the house. He was holding a bloody handkerchief to his thigh and breathing quite heavily. Without hesitation Jennie ran inside for some water and another clean rag. Handing him the cup, she waited until he drank his fill before turning her attention to his wound. There was a lot of blood, and she winched when he reacted in pain to her ministrations with the rag. A moment later another soldier came and knelt beside the two of them. "I'll take it from here, ma'am, you'd best go back inside."

But Jennie didn't go back inside. Instead she grabbed the water bucket and busily doled out a dipper of cool water to all those passing by. Before long she was soaked through, just like the day before. Knowing her skirt couldn't possibly get any dirtier, she ignored the additional caked on mud, and continued her errand of mercy. As always, Jack's image appeared in every face before her, young or old, blonde, black or grey haired, freckled or fair skinned, it didn't matter. She did this for him, and because The Good Book says that 'in whatsoever ye do, do all to the glory of God.' All too soon, however, the firing increased once more and Jennie was forced back inside the house.

For the rest of the day and into the night, the soldiers kept up their constant shooting, firing upon everything that moved in the streets. No one or nothing was safe, even down to horses, chickens, hogs and dogs. Harry and Isaac stayed under the bed, for the most part. Georgia saw to her newborn baby, and Jennie and her mother spent a great deal of their time in the kitchen.

Darkness settled on the small burg in Pennsylvania, and the Wade family attempted to get some much needed rest. Dinner consisted of fresh bread, apple butter, hardboiled eggs, and tea. Hot as it was, in an attempt at normalcy they gathered around the small kitchen table to eat their meager meal and pretend as if a major battle was not taking place all around them. Holding hands, they said their dinner prayer, not neglecting to pray for those going without a meal tonight and for the soldiers still fighting outside.

When they were finished and dishes were cleaned and put away, Jennie glanced down at the box holding what was left of the wood for the stove. There were only three or four small pieces, and she shook her head over how much they had gone through today with all of the baking. Mrs. Wade noticed her look.

"Don't give it another thought, dear. We're completely out of yeast anyway. There will be no more bread coming out of that oven tonight."

Jennie rubbed her aching back. "You know, Mama, I'm almost glad. I don't know how much more of this I can take. But I know there's still plenty more out in the woodpile in back. I can go out there in the morning and bring some more in. We certainly don't need any to keep us warm tonight!"

"That is for certain!"

Mother and daughter joined the others in the front parlor. Harry and Isaac were snuggled under the bed, trying to sleep. Georgia was in bed, the baby tucked up close and sleeping soundly. A small sofa stood beneath a window at the foot of the bed and Jennie lay down on it, fully clothed. Mrs. Wade took a spot on the bed with her daughter and grandson. She, too, slept with her clothes on.

It seemed as if they were barely nodding off when a loud knocking woke them all up. Jennie jumped, not sure what it was she had heard or where it was coming from. Sounds of battle were still going on all around the house and she wasn't sure if another missile woke her or just what it was. The knocking started again, more insistent this time. It was coming from the back door, off the kitchen, and Jennie hurried to answer it before it woke the rest of the sleeping household. Pushing wayward strands of hair from her face, she opened the door slowly. Two soldiers, not much older than herself stood on the stoop, hats in hand.

"We're sorry to bother you, but we heard that you had

some of the best bread in these here parts. You wouldn't happen to have any left, would you?"

Weary beyond anything she had ever experienced before, Jennie left the door open while she trudged across the wood floor to the last remaining plate of biscuits. There were only nine biscuits on the platter, just enough for their breakfast in the morning. She glanced back at the soldiers, staring at her now with wide, pleading eyes. Quickly she snatched two for each of them and hurried across the room before she had time to change her mind.

"This is all we have left for now, but if you come back around mid-morning I can promise you some more."

"Thank you kindly. We sure do appreciate it." The two soldiers dashed off the porch, each one of them stuffing a whole biscuit in their mouth. Jennie's eyes widened as it seemed as if they swallowed them without benefit of chewing. An instant later she prayed that no other soldiers came knocking on their door tonight, because she surely didn't know what they would eat for their own breakfast in the morning if any more doe-eyed strangers showed up on their doorstep.

*   *   *   *

    *   *

Wesley sat in a ditch formed by the making of protective breastworks only several hours old. He was being held in reserves, a spot he had often hated in the past. He hated it for its boredom, and the way it made him feel useless, even hopelessly inadequate to the task. He hated listening to the sounds of battle, the way it shifted from one side of the battlefield to the other, sometimes forward and back. He hated listening to the screams of the wounded, or worse yet, the ones that made no sound at all when being carried to the rear. But this time was worse than any other battle, and he had seen his share of battles. This time the breastworks that shielded him were on the slope of a hill that bore his family name, and the shells of destruction were falling on fields and streets that he used to roam as a boy. He had no idea what time it was, only that the sun had set a long time ago. One thing was for certain, the sounds of battle seemed to be subsiding, with only small pockets of gun fire erupting here and there.

A small branch shifted in the breastworks Wesley had been leaning against, poking him in the back. Pushing himself away, he searched for a better position, something without any rocks or protruding sticks. But as soon as he moved a small avalanche of dirt cascaded down, and he had to hurry to refill the gap.

"Watch it there, Wes! You trying to get us all killed?" Wesley didn't recognize the voice in the dark, but he was sorely temped to share a few words with whoever it was, and maybe even more than mere words. Get them all killed, indeed. Who was that guy kidding? Like this flimsy barrier was going to stop that onslaught of Yankee fire they had been listening to most of the day. Besides, they were in the reserves, far removed from the actual battle itself.

When the breastworks had been repaired, thanks to the help of Ned and Ben, his most trusted friends of late, Wesley found himself another comfortable spot. "Hey, Ned, what time do you suppose it is," he thought to ask.

"I don't rightly know, but I heard someone say it was around ten o'clock a little while ago. Why do you ask?"

"I got something on my mind, something I gotta do. Where do you suppose the captain is?"

"Last I seen him, he was down at the other end of the

works talking to them boys that a was trying to build themselves a fire to cook their dinner over. Can you believe that? Bullets a whizzing all over the place, the enemy on the high ground directly over there, and those idiots want to build a fire. I guess they were just trying to make it easier on those poor Yankees who have had to work so hard all day, loading and reloading their rifles just so they could take pock shots at us. Kind of brings a tear to your eye just a thinking about them, doesn't it?"

Wesley didn't answer. Jack's letter was burning a hole in his pocket, and something told him if he didn't get moving he might never get another opportunity to deliver it. "I gotta go find the captain. I'll be back later." Wesley crouched low and hurried to the other end of the breastworks, in the direction Ned had pointed. Ned called after him, but Wesley didn't turn back, focused instead on his mission.

Finding the captain wasn't as hard as Wesley had thought it might be. Pulling him aside, he explained his plight. As it was, he didn't have to explain much. There was hardly a man in the unit that didn't know the significance between Gettysburg and Wesley. On the other hand, no one knew about the letter in his pocket. Had that little detail come out they might not have been so accommodating about his going into town. These days there weren't too many southerners who were willing to do favors, deathbed wishes or not, for a Yankee. But sneaking into town to visit ones sisters was another matter altogether. Wesley counted the favor a favor, accepted the written pass, and hurried off into the night.

The musket in his hand suddenly felt much lighter, his steps quicker as he made his way through the woods, across a small stream, and into the streets of Gettysburg. Here he had to slow down, making his way cautiously from one house to the next. It was hard to tell which houses were vacant and which might have held sleeping families, as they were all dark and lifeless tonight. By day he knew the streets were a death trap, a perfect opportunity for snipers on either side to pick off any unsuspecting soul that thought to wander away from the shelter of solid walls. But tonight, in the dark, if he was careful and ran fast, he could easily make it all the way to Middle Street, where Annie and Julia lived.

Creeping from one house to the next, he finally made it to the corner of his sister's home. Directly across the street was the Skelly household, the home of Jack's parents. It looked deserted, unwelcoming, like all of the rest of the homes in town. He told himself not to take it personally, that there were probably doors that would open to him even today, even with his wearing of the grey uniform, but now was not the time. Wesley was well aware of the ghosts that had been following him ever since entering the woods on Culp's Hill. But the ghosts were very comforting, not haunting, finger pointing vile beings bent on showing him the evil of his ways. Instead, they were like small recollections getting larger and more vibrant with every turn, every step he took along the way. He could almost hear Jack's voice calling him from the middle of the street to come out and play, or Jennie's constant giggling every time they were up to some childhood mischief. The swirl of memories enveloped him, giving him strength and courage to creep from the shadows and climb the steps to his sister's front door.

Suddenly aware of his appearance, he removed his kepi, using it to knock at the dust and dirt of his uniform. The rain barrel was visible just round the corner of the house, where it had always stood, and quickly Wesley dashed down the steps, hoping against hope that there would be enough in it for a quick wipe-down. Sticking his hand inside the wooden barrel, he was thrilled to find it more than half full. Quickly a hankie was pulled from his jacket pocket and dunked into the barrel, and a few minutes later he felt like a new man. His face and hands were clean, and his hair slicked back from his forehead. He was ready now to meet his sister's.

Slowly he made his way back up to the door, not knowing where the nervousness came from. He knew without a doubt that he would be welcome, but it had been years since he had seen them, and they him. Perhaps it was the uncertainty of change or preconceived expectations that had his hand frozen over the door, unable to knock. Water dripped from his soaked coat sleeve, crickets, heedless of the day's battle, hummed their nighttime song, and somewhere a horse neighed. Wesley took a deep breath, and before he knew what was happening his knuckles were rapping on the wooden door.

There was movement on the other side of the door, and a female voice called out. "Who's there?"

Afraid to speak up too loudly, Wesley croaked out an answer. "It's Wesley. Open up."

The door opened so quickly, Wesley was momentarily startled. But when Annie reached out an arm to yank him inside he had to laugh out loud.

"Oh, brother, it is so good to see you!" The door had barely closed behind him when he found himself locked in a tight embrace.

His younger sister, Julia, just entering the room, seemed as shocked as he was when the door first opened on him. And like his initial shock, it was momentary, because seconds later she was bounding across the floor and wrapping her arms around both Annie and himself, locking them all in an even tighter embrace.

No one seemed to want to be the first one to let go. But it was Annie who put a stop to the screaming and laughter. "Come! Come, that's enough now! We don't want the whole neighborhood, or what's left of it, to hear us and come running to investigate." And with that, the two women stepped back, the better to study their long, lost brother.

"Oh, Wes, you look…you look…"

"I know, I look awful, but that's what comes of marching all day and sleeping under the stars at night."

"No, not at all. I was going to say that you look wonderful, a sight for these sore eyes." It was Annie that was doing all of the talking. Julia hadn't said a word since he walked, or rather, was dragged into the room. Instead, she constantly dabbed at her eyes with the corner of her hankie.

Seemingly unable to keep her hands off of her brother, Annie once more grabbed Wesley by the arm. "Come, let's go into the kitchen where we might be free from prying eyes. Besides, you look like you could use something to eat. Am I right?"

"Well, I know one thing's for sure, I can't remember the last time I was so man-handled!"

Both women laughed at that, while they ceremoniously dragged out the head chair, forcing him into it. Julia finally came to herself, apologizing that they didn't have a lot to eat, while busily bringing up a plate of biscuits, jam, applesauce, and cheese. In between bites, he did his best to get them caught up on all that had transpired in his life since they last met. For hours they sat around that kitchen table, soaking up Wesley's stories the way he soaked up every speck of jam from his plate.

Most of Wesley's stories were of camp life, or marches that took him from one side of a state to another, of sleeping on the ground in rain, snow and warm summer evenings, of food that wasn't fit for hogs but that they ate it anyway because it was either that or starve altogether. He left out all mention of battle scenes, including the one currently taking place. His sister's sat mesmerized, barely shifting in their chairs long enough to cross one ankle over the other.

All too soon, it seemed, it was time for Wesley to think about leaving. It was then that he decided to bring up the subject of Jack. "I was in Winchester a few weeks back, when they had that battle. Did you hear about it?"

"Did we hear about it? Why, it was the talk of the town for weeks! Some of our own boys were in that battle, and some of them didn't make it, we hear." Annie fell silent then, the awkwardness of talking to her brother, who was on one side of the war, and referring to hometown boys, of which he was one, but meaning the other side of the war, making things rather difficult to explain. Her sentiments were with the boys of Gettysburg and the Union, but her heart was still with her brother, whatever uniform he might be wearing.

Wesley offered a sad smile. He knew exactly what she meant.

"You didn't happen to see anyone we know, did you?" There was an underlying fear in Annie's question. The idea that if Wesley did happen upon a local boy he would be forced to fire upon him, making the answer all the more painful.

"Well, as a matter of fact, I did."

Wesley heard Julia's slight intake of breath, and there was a slight hesitation before Annie spoke again. "Really? Who was it?"

"It was after the fighting actually. We were gathering up the wounded and the prisoners and suddenly I hear this voice, from amidst the prisoners, calling my name. When I turned around I saw Billy Holzworth waving his arms at me. He had Jack with him."

"Not Jack Skelly? That Jack?"

"Was he all right?"

"Was he wounded?"

The questions were being fired faster than Wesley could answer them. Suddenly he held up his hands as if to hold off a physical barrage. "Just let me finish, all right?"

"Oh, yes, sorry. You go right ahead."

"As I was saying, Billy called me over and showed me how Jack had been hit in the shoulder. He was bleeding quite badly and needed some help."

Both women gasped.

"And, of course, Billy was hoping that I could hurry and get Jack to a doctor or a hospital or something. I have to admit, it was hard seeing him under these circumstances. Billy, too, because he was being marched off to a prisoner of war camp someplace and there was nothing I could do about that. But Jack

I could help. I managed to get him toted into town where they had several hospitals set up to receive the wounded from both sides. I even went to see him later. He was at the Taylor House with a bunch of other wounded, and not looking good at all."

"Oh, poor, dear Jack. The Skelly's are going to be so upset by this news."

"When last I saw him he was sitting up in bed with a big old bandage over his shoulder. He asked me to deliver a letter for someone in town for him. I have it right here in my jacket pocket." Wesley patted his upper pocket for effect.

"For someone in town, you say? That someone wouldn't happen to be a young lady we all know, would it?" Annie raised her eyebrows, looking at Wesley inquiringly.

Julia couldn't hide the smile that was lighting up her face. "Tell us, Wes. Who's the letter for?"

"It's not for me to say. But I promised to deliver it, and deliver it I shall." At that Wesley rose to his feet.

The women were quick to jump to theirs as well, Annie almost knocking over her chair in the bargain. "You're not leaving so soon? Why you just got here! Won't you spend the night with us? You can always go back in the morning."

"I'm sorry, Annie, but I can't, much as I'd like to. I have to get this letter delivered and get back before daylight. Darkness is the only thing that will keep me safe until I reach behind our lines once more. The Yankees are all over the place out there, and some of my own men might fire on me if I get caught in town now."

"But you just got here, and we might never see you again." Annie continued pleading her case, but it was no use. Wesley knew that this was not a safe place for him to be, that some of his own relatives and old neighbors had threatened to shoot him on the spot if they saw him. And if the Yankees were to find him here, it could go badly for Annie and Julia.

"I wish I could stay, I really do, but I have to get moving on." Grabbing up his musket, Wesley headed for the door.

"Wait," cried Annie, slipping the remaining biscuits into a sack and handing it to him. "You might need these later."

No more words were said as throats tightened up, and words refused to come. Quietly Wesley opened the door and disappeared into the night. The two women stood at the door, listening to the last of his footsteps fade into the dark.

Stealthily Wesley made his way through several backyards, across High Street, and through more backyards until he came across the Wade household on Breckenridge Street. Like all of the other houses in town, this one was dark. But, unlike all of the other houses, this one had the back door wide open. Wesley crept closer, into the large lilac bush that grew beside the back stoop. Its fragrant blooms were long gone, like childhood dreams and wishes. But it wasn't the sweet floral scent he was looking for tonight, merely cover from whoever might be inside that house. It wasn't like the Wade family to leave their door open for any and all to enter, especially under these circumstances. But as Wesley made it to the very door of the house he distinctly heard footsteps within, heavy footsteps, as if from Yankee brogans. Crouching deeper within the lilac bush, Wesley waited, listening for sounds other than footsteps, sounds that would confirm the identity of those who made the very footsteps that gave him pause in the first place. He didn't have long to wait. Within minutes he heard male laughter, quickly followed by a voice so thick with a Yankee accent he could have sliced it like a wedge of cheese.

Jack's letter crinkled in his pocket, the slight noise heard only by himself. But it was enough to remind him that he was still in possession of the missive, that he hadn't delivered it into Jennie's hands yet. A chair scraped across the floor inside the house, and a Yankee soldier coughed. Without another thought, Wesley dove from the sanctuary of the lilac bush, around the corner of the house and into another backyard bordering on Baltimore Street. There he spotted two more soldiers, also Yankee, sitting on the ground, their backs propped up against the side of a building, sharing a smoke. For the first time Wesley knew terror within the confines of his own hometown. Never before had these streets offered him anything but a place to play, to grow, to learn. His situation was precarious, his only protection the night and the side of an outhouse he was leaning against. Closing his eyes, he forced his breathing to calm down, his heart rate to slow. He had to think!

There had to be a way back to his uncle's farm on Culp's Hill that wouldn't take him directly into the path of a Yankee musket ball. He, Jack and Jennie had done it thousands of times, escaping chores, the last day of school, angry parents or siblings, or any other number of reasons why children would want to run to the hills or woods that circled this town. Calm now, he opened his eyes, and as if Jack and Jennie were holding onto his hands leading him back to safety, Wesley unerringly made his way out of town towards the hill that bore his family name, and where his friends waited for him. Along the way he passed by a two-story brick home that he, Jack and Jennie had always thought looked odd. It looked like a house all right, but it was divided right down the middle so that two families could live in it at the same time, one on one side and another family on the other. They used to shake their heads at the prospect when they would go visit Jennie's grandparents, who lived not too far away. Tonight he gave it no more than a cursory glance, it being dark like everything else in town. Besides, there were plenty of Yankees in the vicinity, urging him into a faster pace.

Shortly after midnight Wesley made it back into the ditch behind the breastworks. Ned and Ben both slapped him on the back. "Glad to see you made it back!"

"Did you have a good time with your sisters?"

Wesley felt the weight of the letter in his pocket. Folded up tightly and close to his heart, that thin sheet of paper was all that stood between him and a perfect call on his family. It tainted the whole visit! Returning his friend's warm welcome, Wesley didn't want his disappointment to show. Instead, he smiled, told him that he had a wonderful time, and brought out the several biscuits that Annie had shoved into his hand at the last moment. They accepted them with relish, and the three friends finished them in silence before lying down to get some sleep. But sleep didn't come easy for Wesley that night, the letter and the broken promise laying heavy on his conscience. Flat on his back, he pulled the kepi low over his face, and willed sleep to come. All too soon he heard Ned softly snoring beside him. Wounded were somewhere close by, because he could hear their moans and sometimes sharp cries of pain. And somewhere a small animal found its end in the talons of some night bird of prey, its screams piercing the night, not unlike the broken promise that pierced Wesley's soul.

Chapter 11

Gettysburg

Friday, July 3, 1863

"and God shall wipe away all tears from their eyes;
and there shall be no more death, neither sorrow, nor crying,
neither shall there be any more pain;
for the former things are passed away."
Revelation 21:4

Dawn stole silently upon the broken little town of Gettysburg. With the first faint rays of sun came the heralding of every type and species of bird still in the area. Singing out their morning song, they loudly heralded the arrival of still another day, singing their praises to the Creator of all. Mere seconds later another sound rent the air, louder even than the birds, and in sharp contrast to their heavenly chorus. It was the sound of cannon, shot and shell. In no time, everyone was awake for miles around, as death and destruction visited them all again.

Someone kicked Wesley's legs, and moved on down the line.

"Wake up! Get up, all of you! There's work to be done now boys! Today we take that hill and drive those blasted Yanks all the way back to Kingdom Come! Come on now, get moving!"

There were groans, and not a few remarks about their first cup of coffee, but all of them were soon on their feet. Climbing out from behind the safety of their breastworks the men charged up the hill. Yankee bullets met them before they made it twenty feet. Instantly they dove for whatever cover they could find, returning fire when able. All too quickly the woods were filled with smoke, making it hard to see where to go or what, precisely, to shoot at.

The company flag was off to Wesley's left, and as much as was possible he kept it in his sights. Communication was near impossible as Yankee cannon tore through the trees overhead, sending branches and debris raining down upon them. There was no safe place any more! Wesley watched in horror as one cannon ball ripped clean through a tree that Ben was using as protection. Barley two feet of trunk was left standing, behind which Ben still crouched. Under other circumstances the look on his face would have been completely comical, but not today, not on this day filled with life or death matters. Wordlessly Wesley watched as Ben took a few deep breaths, shaking it off. Together they sprang from their hiding place, racing for another boulder of which Culp's Hill was so famous. It took them only seconds to reload their muskets and press on with the rest of their company.

The firing was intense, and Wesley was surprised to glance around periodically and not see more men going down. Reloading still again he began to think that what he heard about these Yankee marksmen was true, that they were horrible! Perhaps there was hope for this southern army yet! Maybe they will be enjoying Sunday dinner in Washington City!

All of these thoughts gave Wesley courage, chasing away what remained of the cobwebs of sleep, and spurring him on to greater challenges. Slowly his company made their way blindly way up the hill, one rock after another, one tree after another. It was slow going, but they were making obvious progress, and at no time did they suffer a retreat.

In all the turmoil he had lost track of Ned, but Ben was still by his side. He waited until Ben was ready, gave the signal, and both of them charged out from behind their latest barricade, a huge tree recently felled by Yankee cannon. With a might scream they ran headlong up the hill. Suddenly Wesley felt a tugging at the breast pocket of his sack coat, where Jack's letter lay safely tucked away. Falling to the ground, his hand went protectively there, and came away wet with blood. Dumfounded, he stared at it for several seconds, wondering what it all meant. Before comprehension could sink in, Wesley Culp breathed his last on the hill that bore his name. His sightless eyes stared up through the smoke enshrouded treetops all the way to the deep expanse of Heaven itself. His hand still clutched the pocket, now torn and bleeding all over Jack's letter. The next thing he knew someone was trying to take his hand, the very one that was still protecting that letter. When he looked he realized that it was Jack, Jack himself!

He cried out. "Oh, Jack! Jack, I'm so sorry! I tried to deliver it, I really did, but she wasn't home last night while I was in town. I didn't know what else to do. Jack, I'm so sorry."

But Jack simply shook his head as if it didn't matter at all, urging Wesley to his feet. Surprisingly Wesley realized how weightless he felt, rising effortlessly from the ground. Not only that, but he and Jack didn't stop when rising to their feet, but kept rising above the battle that still raged all around them, the bullets, shot and shell heedlessly flying all around them.

"Come with me, Wesley, there's someone you really need to meet."

"But Jack, what about the letter?"

"Forget about the letter, Wes. You're the best friend in the world for trying to deliver it for me, but there is someone you need to meet now. Someone who has been waiting a long time to welcome you home."

Jack let go of Wesley's hand just then, letting him stand on his own merit. It was then he realized they were surrounded by hundreds of thousands of figures in white, all singing the most lovely Alleluja chorus he had every heard. The hunger he felt when he first woke up was forgotten, as were his sore, bare feet. He no longer felt grubby, bug infested, or in need of a bath, and it never occurred him to question any of it. Closing his eyes to the wonder of it all, he soaked up the lovely singing of the angelic chorus. Suddenly their singing got louder, more focused, and Wesley opened his eyes to discover why. And there in their midst stood Jesus, his arms outstretched and welcoming Wesley with more love than Wesley thought possible, or ever dared to imagine. It didn't occur to him at first to wonder how he recognized Jesus, never having seen Him before, but as Jack led him forward, it all suddenly made perfect sense. Jack was the one who had introduced him to Jesus in the first place! All those years ago, when they were kids growing up in Gettysburg he had dragged Wesley to church and Sunday School with him, never taking no for an answer. He kept saying, 'one of these days you'll find out why,' and Wesley finally found out what he meant. It was then that Wesley realized his hand was still over his heart, over a hole that was no longer there. The letter was at last forgotten, and everything paled in comparison to standing before His King.

*   *   *   *
*

At dawn the sound of a violent thunderstorm woke Jennie from a restless sleep. Startled, she sat bolt upright, then realized it wasn't thunder at all. It was the sound of cannon, musket, and rifle fire south of the house, near Culp's Hill. The battle had started again.

From her spot on the sofa beneath the window, Jennie looked across the room towards Georgia. Her sister never looked more tired as she laid in bed, the baby tucked in close beside her. The usual greeting of, "did you sleep well," died on her lips as her sister groaned against the rude awakening.

"Well, might as well get at it, I guess," their mother said, looking as tired as the rest. Still fully dressed, she swung her legs over the side of the bed, mindful of stepping on the boys who may or may not be sticking legs or arms out from beneath the bed where they had spent the night.

Mrs. Wade called to them, softly, just in case. She found them awake, like everyone else now, but unsure of what to do. All routine had faded from their lives when the soldiers entered into it.

Wiping the sleep from her eyes, Mrs. Wade glanced across the room to Jennie. "Come, child, we best get busy at those biscuits you promised the men yesterday. You know they could be here any minute now." As she walked past Jennie's bed towards the kitchen, her hand gently tugged her daughter's sleeve. "This is all your doing, you know." But there was no recrimination in her tone, and only a smile on her lips. Jennie smiled back, knowing her mother would have promised nothing less to the men in blue.

"Coming, Mama. I'll just go get some wood for the fire. Harry, why don't you help me?" Jennie adjusting the bodice of her dress and smoothed her apron, doing her best to make herself presentable. Harry got to his feet, wiped the sleep from his eyes and followed his sister to the door.

"You two be careful out there and stick close to the house. Those boys are at it already this morning, God forbid." Mrs. Wade scooped ashes from the stove, dumping them in a bucket that would be emptied later.

Jennie and Harry had no trouble gathering up a load of firewood for the stove. The soldiers had generously chopped and piled wood for them around the corner of the house and up against the wall. It was their way of making sure they might get fresh bread and biscuits when they wanted them. Grabbing one more piece of firewood, Jennie quickly ushered them both back inside the house. They barely made it through the back door before the sound of rifle fire seemed to escalate on the hill.

The house was already incredibly warm, but they didn't dare leave the door open for ventilation for fear of wayward bullets. Georgia was sitting up in bed now, nursing tiny Louis. Isaac had crawled out from beneath the bed and was sitting up in the corner, still out of everyone's way, but better able to see what was going on. Harry went over to join him.

Jennie joined her mother in the kitchen, which promised to get hotter as the day wore on. Together they measured the dry ingredients for a fresh batch of biscuits. Jennie's back was to the door, when suddenly a knock sounded. Both women jumped, screaming involuntarily. When they realized it was nothing more than the first soldier of the day, they laughed and let out a sigh of relief.

"Frayed nerves," Mrs. Wade mumbled, going back to her measuring.

Jennie wiped her hands on her apron and turned to answer the door. A young soldier stood on the threshold. He was dirty, like all the rest. In one hand he held his cap respectfully, revealing unkempt hair that hadn't seen soap and water in weeks. In the other was an Enfield rifle, held at his side like a staff, the butt resting on the ground. "Sorry to disturb, Miss, but some of the fella's said you was to have some of the best biscuits they'd eatin in quite a spell. I was wonderin' if you might have any more to spare?"

Jennie's heart went out to the young soldier. "Well, I'm sorry, but we're all out right now." She didn't miss the slight drooping of the young man's shoulders. "But don't worry. My mother and I are busy whipping up another batch this very minute. If you could come back in about an hour, I'll make sure you get some of the first ones out of the oven. How will that be?"

The soldier's eyes lit up at the suggestion and a smile immediately spread across his face. "Thank you kindly, Miss," he said with a bow. "I'll be sure to come back." The sounds of battle hovered in the air as the soldier disappeared around the corner of the house, towards the cemetery. Jennie closed the door, hoping he would live to taste the biscuits when they were done.

"There's coffee, dear," her mother said, offering her a cup. "Why don't we sit down for a few minutes and enjoy a bit of breakfast ourselves. There isn't much, just some bread, butter and applesauce, but we'll make do, won't we?"

At the mention of food, both Harry and Isaac called out from the sitting room. "We're hungry, too! Can we have some bread and applesauce, please?"

Jennie and her mother exchanged looks. "Some things never change," Mrs. Wade uttered. But there was no contempt in her voice as she handed Jennie a plate to take in to the boys. "You go ahead, I'll fix one for Georgia and be right with you."

The boys huddled together on a blanket in the corner of the room, listening to sounds of the ongoing battle. Isaac especially jerked every time one blast seemed louder than the last. They had made quick use of the bread and applesauce, but the coffee didn't seem to hold much appeal for them this morning.

Jennie reached for her Bible. "Why don't I do some reading out loud. Would you like that," she asked the room in general. Harry voiced his approval, which Isaac immediately echoed. Mrs. Wade lifted her coffee cup in assent. Only Georgia seemed preoccupied, holding little Louis tightly and glancing around the room as if she expected bullets to come flying through the very walls at any moment.

Jennie could certainly understand such fears. Didn't she herself flinch involuntarily when one blast sounded closer or louder than the one before? Slowly her hands caressed the smooth leather of the Bible cover. Her mind wandered, as unseeing eyes drifted across thin, fragile pages full of words waiting to comfort and soothe an anxious soul. Jack's face loomed before her, and she wondered where he was. She hadn't heard from him in months. And though others told her not to worry, that mail delivery was unreliable these days, especially now that the war had come to the north, she couldn't help it. There was a sort of heaviness to her heart, a persistent nagging she could not define beyond a woman's intuition that told her something wasn't quite right. And she knew she wouldn't be able to rest until she finally heard from Jack.

Georgia was experiencing the same torment over her husband of just over a year. The last they heard from him he was heading towards Richmond to try and overtake the Confederate capital once again, but that was weeks ago. A lot can happen in a week during wartime, as they all knew only too well.

And what of their brother, John? Was it only days ago that she had mended his uniform and sent him on his way to battle? Where was he now, their other brave soldier in blue? Did he make it safely out of town to his own lines, or wasn't there any such thing as safe any more?

"Jennie, when are you going to start reading to us?" Harry asked, sitting on the blanket, knees pulled up tight against his chest.

"Yeah, we like it when you read from the Bible!" mimicked Isaac.

Jennie blinked several times to clear her head of blue and grey uniforms and faces she might never see again. The slight smell of gunpowder infiltrated the house, and Jennie tried to ignore it like she was ignoring the sounds of battle themselves. Glancing down, she saw that the Bible had opened up to the Psalms, as good a place to start as any. Crossing her legs, Jennie positioned the Good Book comfortably on her lap. She read aloud, "Psalm 27, verse one, 'The Lord is my light and my salvation; whom shall I fear? The Lord is the strength of my life, of whom shall I be afraid?" The encouraging words brought her comfort, strengthening her resolve to face the day and the calamity outside. Her chin rose higher, and her voice took on more confidence. "Though a host should encamp against me, my heart shall not fear..."

"Mama, make her stop," Georgia suddenly pleaded. "Make her find something else to read. I don't like where this is going."

Jennie glanced up, but only momentarily. Her mother hadn't spoke in rebuke, so Jennie continued on. "Though war should rise against me..."

"Mama, please!" Enraged, Georgia sat up straighter. Louis felt her anxiety and cried out in protest. "I don't want to hear any more talk about war. I cannot!"

Mrs. Wade took the coffee cup away from her lips in agitation. "Georgia, calm yourself. You're not doing the baby or anyone else in this room any good with your outburst."

"But, Mama..."

"And Jennie, dear, why don't you find something of a more cheerful nature. The Psalms are full of lovely, uplifting verses. Or you could read something from the Gospels, if you prefer. But please do stop reading about war."

Feeling the sting of chastisement, but mollified that her mother had at least demanded Jennie stop all talk of war, Georgia resettled herself on the bed, and worked to calm the now red-faced infant.

Jennie continued. "Let me just finish this chapter, 'Wait on the Lord; be of good courage, and He shall strengthen thine heart." She closed the Book with a flourish, a contented smile on her face. "That was better, was it not?" Before anyone could utter anything in response, a shower of bullets suddenly struck the house. Before anyone had time to respond splinters of glass from the broken windows fell like snow upon the wooden floor. The two boys dodged beneath the bed in panic. Jennie and her mother screamed and fell to the ground. Meanwhile Georgia squirmed her way deep into the mattress, an arm outstretched to cover the form of her screaming infant. For several minutes nobody moved, fearful that the volley of musket balls would begin again.

Mrs. Wade rose first, quick, darting glances taking in the damage to windows and wall alike. Not a pane of glass was left unshattered.

"Is everyone all right," she called out.

Trembling voices came from beneath the bed. "Yes, ma'am."

Jennie didn't answer her mother, but their eyes locked, and she knew her youngest daughter was none the worse for wear.

It was Georgia that had them both concerned. She had not answered, nor had she moved a muscle since the attack had stopped. Mrs. Wade moved to the side of the bed, Jennie right beside her. As Jennie called her sister's name, their mother reached across the bed and plucked a bullet from the pillow beside Georgia's head. Hefting it in her hand, she realized it was still warm. The three women stared at the intrusive object, its deadly intent clearly recognizable in the glances passing between them.

Wordlessly Mrs. Wade dropped the piece of lead in her apron pocket.

Georgia brought her newborn son to her breast in a fierce hug of love and protection.

Jennie spun on her heels, heading for the kitchen. But before she left the room, Georgia heard her utter, "If there is anyone in this house that is to be killed today, I hope it's me. Not poor Georgia with that little baby."

Mrs. Wade peaked beneath the bed to check on the boys. When she was satisfied they were shaken, but otherwise all right, she joined Jennie in the kitchen. Nerves frayed to the breaking point, neither woman spoke for several minutes. Instead, they busied themselves in the mechanics of preparing biscuits for the hungry soldiers they knew would soon be knocking on the door. Occasionally their eyes met, and the faint beginnings of a smile would play at the corners of their mouths. Finally, Mrs. Wade asked, "Who's in control, Jennie?"

"God is in control, Mama." They each drew a ragged breath, strengthening their resolve and finding comfort in doing routine kitchen duties.

Bullets continued to wiz by the house, but they no longer seemed to attack the house in general. Throughout the morning soldiers could be heard outside, calling to one another as they ran by the house. The battle was keeping them from making further demands for fresh biscuits. But, Jennie and her mother both knew there would be calls aplenty once the aroma of fresh biscuits began filling the air.

Intent on their mission, the women worked silently in the kitchen. Mrs. Wade opened the cast iron door to the stove, its loud creaking lost in the sounds of the raging battle outside.

Jennie leaned over the table, giving the biscuit dough several last kneads before cutting them up and preparing them for the oven. Each time she leaned forward her apron would brush against the leg of the table, Jack's picture making a slight tapping noise. She smiled as she thought of him trying to get her attention, as if he was ever very far away from her thoughts anyway.

Suddenly that horrible sound of bullet crashing through wood sounded behind her. But before she could comprehend, a stinging pain struck her in the back. There was no time to scream, to think, or even react. In the space of time it took to draw a last breath, Jennie was gone.

Her body hit the floor, lifeless. But for Jennie, life was just beginning. Like Jack and Wesley before her, the sounds of battle quickly gave way to a very persistent, but beautiful angelic chorus, all singing praises to and heralding the arrival of The One whose name is above all other names – Jesus!

Jennie rose to her feet, feeling lighter than any feather. Suddenly she felt as if she could fly by merely wishing it so, but there was no need. Two strong pair of arms, one on each side, pulled her effortlessly to her feet. She looked up se see Jack on one side and Wesley on the other, and it never occurred to her to question any of it. Her heart began to sing, the words coming quickly up and out of her mouth, as she and her two friends joined in the chorus with the angels. She thought the smile on her face couldn't get any wider, and then she looked up and saw – Him! She saw Jesus smiling back at her, and she finally knew what true happiness was when He said, "Well done, my true and faithful servant."

"O Death, where is your sting?"
1 Corinthians 15:55